THE SOUTH AFRICAN
Ostrich Cookbook

First published in 1999 by
Struik Publishers (Pty) Ltd
(a member of Struik New Holland Publishing (Pty) Ltd)
Cornelis Struik House
80 McKenzie Street
Cape Town 8001

Reg. No.: 54/00965/07

2 4 6 8 10 9 7 5 3 1

Editor: Joy Clack
Concept designer: Sonia de Villiers
Designer: Beverley Dodd
Photographer: Ryno
Stylist: Sylvie Hurford
Illustrator: Sonia de Villiers

Reproduction by Disc Express Cape (Pty) Ltd
Printed and bound by Craft Print (Pte) Ltd, Singapore

ISBN 1 86872 381 X

Contents

Foreword

I have enjoyed cooking with ostrich these past twenty years, and was therefore thrilled when asked to write this short foreword for *The South African Ostrich Cookbook*.

As a chef, it's easy to see why ostrich has become so popular in South Africa and, indeed, all over the world. It is full of flavour, low in fat and lends itself to creative cooking. This reminds me of one of the first dishes I cooked using ostrich: I roasted a fillet in the oven after I had crusted it in nibbed almonds and sweet pepper – it was a knockout.

I am happy to say that teams of South African chefs have used ostrich as their main item in culinary competitions all over the world, gaining many gold medals in top-class culinary competitions.

In today's health-conscious world, ostrich can become part of a balanced diet that allows the meat eater the pleasure of enjoying a great steak and knowing that it is a healthy choice.

Grilled, roasted, braised or smoked, ostrich is a versatile product that is not only healthy, but also one of the most tender and tasty meats on the menu. It is the perfect signature dish to promote our 'Rainbow Cuisine' and bring South African foods to the forefront. Keep it cooking!

Dr Bill Gallagher
Chairman – South African Chef's Association
President – World Association of Cooks Societies

A Note from the Authors

To date, only a few cookbooks have been published with recipes and helpful hints for cooking with ostrich. We felt that a comprehensive ostrich cookbook was long overdue and this is our attempt at producing one.

Many of the recipes in the book have been created by award-winning chefs, and we wish to thank the South African Chef's Association for their contributions. Wherever possible, we have given the name of the creator of the recipe. There are too many people to thank individually for their assistance, but we would like to make special mention of Thomas and Charlise Grove of Goblins Cove Restaurant in Hekpoort, who helped to test so many of the recipes. Also a very big thank you to Swartland Ostriches, Ostriches Galore and Oryx Abattoir for donating the meat for the photography.

If you have recipes, hints or tips that you would like to add, we would appreciate hearing from you. You will get full credit in subsequent editions and updates. We can both be contacted via the North West Ostrich Association (Pauline is Chairperson and Danelle is Vice Chairperson) at PO Box 275, Kroondal 0350.

Happy AND HEALTHY cooking!

Pauline Henderson   Danelle Coulson

Historical Information

Ostriches were first domesticated in the late 1700s in the Oudtshoorn area. With the purpose of supplying feathers to European markets, birds were imported from the Barbary States to improve the feather quality.

For most of the last century, the Klein Karoo Landbou Ko-operasie (KKLK) has controlled the ostrich industry in South Africa. The industry was deregulated in 1993 and since then it has exploded. In addition to the many farmers in the Karoo, there are now over 500 ostrich farmers in Gauteng, the Northern and North West Provinces. Ostrich farming has also grown tremendously in the United States and Israel over the past five years and is now starting to take off in many other countries, such as China, Malaysia, Indonesia and even Sweden and Norway. Everyone has come to realize the value of these birds.

Initially the birds were raised for their feathers, but in recent years the demand for ostrich meat and ostrich skin has rapidly increased. Ostrich skin is the second-strongest skin known – only kangaroo is stronger. Skins are sold to leather-goods manufacturers for handbags, shoes, boots, wallets, etc. Ostrich meat is the healthiest red meat in the world because of its low fat content.

An ostrich is the world's largest flightless bird and can grow to a height of 2.75 m (9 ft). It can weigh up to 200 kg (450 lb), live up to 70 years of age, and can run up to 60–70 km/h (40–45 mph). No, they do not bury their heads in the sand. When danger threatens, young birds will stretch out flat with their necks extended and play possum – thus the myth. But, yes, they do eat stones. Ostriches do not have teeth and therefore need stones in their stomachs to help grind up their food.

The Nutritional Value of Ostrich Meat and Basic Cuts

Basic cuts

The prime cuts are fillet and steak. There is also neck, mince, goulash (for stewing and slow cooking), liver and tripe. Fillet is the tenderest cut. There are also many processed ostrich meat varieties, from smoked fillet to pastrami, pâté, biltong and dried sausage (droëwors).

NOTE: If cooked too long (well done), ostrich meat will become dry. Prepare steaks and fillet to medium-rare.

Nutritional value

Ostrich is a red meat that has a much lower fat count than chicken, turkey, beef, lamb and pork. It has not only become a healthy alternative to red meat, but its distinct, subtle taste and versatility have made it sought after by hoteliers, restaurateurs, home cooks and caterers throughout the world.

A comparison table follows:

Nutritional Information per 100g raw, extra-trim meat (trimmed of all visible fat)			
	Energy Value (kJ)	Protein (g)	Fat (g)
Ostrich			
Steak	388 kJ	21.1 g	0.8 g
Fillet	392 kJ	21.3 g	0.8 g
Stir-fry	388 kJ	21.1 g	0.8 g
Beef			
Rump Steak	504 kJ	19.0 g	4.90 g
Fillet	543 kJ	19.0 g	5.95 g
Stir-fry	564 kJ	19.0 g	6.50 g
Pork			
Steak	468 kJ	19.5 g	3.70 g
Fillet	498 kJ	19.5 g	4.50 g
Stir-fry	498 kJ	19.5 g	4.50 g
Chicken			
Breasts (deboned)	458 kJ	21.5 g	2.50 g
Stir-fry	458 kJ	21.5 g	2.50 g
Lamb			
Stir-fry	619 kJ	19.0 g	8.00 g

Compiled by Pick 'n Pay Butcheries, July 1998.
For more information, contact the Health Hotline on (011) 456-2626.

Soups & Starters

SOUPS

Ostrich-neck Soup (1)

Serves 6

1 ostrich neck, cut into pieces
1 large onion, chopped
1.5 litres (2¾ pints) water
250 ml (1 cup) diced carrots
250 ml (1 cup) diced potatoes
4 stalks parsley
125 ml (½ cup) diced tomato
60 ml (4 tbsp) port
7 ml (1½ tsp) Worcestershire sauce
salt and freshly ground black pepper to taste

Place the neck and all the vegetables in the water and bring to the boil. Simmer for 4 hours.

Add the port, Worcestershire sauce and seasoning half an hour before serving.

SOURCE UNKNOWN

Ostrich-neck Soup (2)

Serves 6

100 ml (3½ fl oz) cooking oil
1 kg (2¼ lb) ostrich neck, sliced
1 large onion, coarsely sliced
1 packet brown onion soup
1 carrot, diced
1 stalk celery, chopped
Bouquet garni in muslin bag
1 x 410 g (14 oz) tin chopped tomatoes
freshly ground pepper and salt to taste
1.5 litres (2½ pints) water
100 ml (3½ fl oz) sherry or wine (optional)

Heat the oil in a heavy-based pot. Add the neck and brown, then add the onion. Braise until soft. Add all the remaining ingredients, except the wine, and simmer for 4 hours or until the meat is falling off the bones. Add more water if necessary.

Remove the bones from the soup. Be careful – ostrich neck has some tiny bones that tend to get left behind. Add the wine or sherry and simmer for another 15 minutes. Check seasoning and serve with fresh bread.

CHRIS PATON
PRETORIA

Chilli Goulash Soup

Serves 6

500 g (1 lb 2 oz) ostrich goulash
2 large onions, chopped
30 ml (2 tbsp) chilli powder (or to taste)
salt and freshly ground black pepper to taste
3 litres (5¼ pints) water
500 g (1 lb 2 oz) carrots, chopped
1 x 410 g (14 oz) tin peas

Combine the ostrich, onions, chilli powder, salt, pepper and water in a large pot and bring to the boil. Reduce heat and simmer for 2 hours. Add the carrots and simmer for another 45 minutes. Add the peas a few minutes before serving.

SOURCE UNKNOWN

Taco Soup

Serves 6

45 ml (3 tbsp) oil
1 kg (2¼ lb) ostrich mince
2 fresh red chillies, seeded and diced
1 onion, diced
500 ml (2 cups) peeled, seeded and diced tomatoes
750 ml (1¼ pints) ostrich stock
(see recipe on page 11)
500 ml (18 fl oz) tomato juice
15 ml (1 tbsp) cumin
15 ml (1 tbsp) chilli powder
5 ml (1 tsp) salt
tortilla chips
375 ml (1½ cups) grated Cheddar cheese

In a large pot, heat the oil and brown the ostrich mince. Add the chillies and onion and sauté until tender. Add the tomatoes, stock, tomato juice and seasonings. Bring to the boil, reduce heat and simmer for 15 minutes.

Pour the soup into bowls, garnish with tortillas and cheese and serve.

SOURCE UNKNOWN

Ostrich Minestrone Milanese

Serves 8

1 ostrich neck
45 ml (3 tbsp) butter
1 garlic clove, crushed
125 ml (½ cup) sliced onion
125 ml (½ cup) diced celery
125 ml (½ cup) diced green pepper
125 ml (½ cup) sliced mushrooms
125 ml (½ cup) diced baby marrows
3 medium potatoes, peeled and diced
500 ml (2 cups) peeled, seeded and diced tomatoes
10 ml (2 tsp) Worcestershire sauce
5 ml (1 tsp) dried basil
2 ml (½ tsp) dried thyme
2 ml (½ tsp) dried oregano
5 ml (1 tsp) salt
500 ml (2 cups) cooked penne noodles
45 ml (3 tbsp) freshly grated Parmesan cheese

Simmer the ostrich neck in 2 litres (3½ pints) water in a covered pot for 3–4 hours or until the meat falls off the bone. Strain and reserve the liquid. Remove the meat from the bones and put to one side. Be careful not to leave any small bones behind.

Heat the butter in a large pot. Add the garlic, onion, celery, green pepper, mushrooms and baby marrows and sauté until tender. Add the potatoes and tomatoes and sauté for 5 minutes.

Pour 1.25 litres (2¼ pints) of the reserved stock into the pot, along with 500 ml (2 cups) of the meat. (Any leftover meat can be used for another dish that requires cooked ostrich.) Add the Worcestershire sauce, basil, thyme, oregano and salt. Simmer gently for 15–20 minutes or until the potatoes are cooked yet firm.

Stir in the noodles and cheese and cook for a further 2 minutes.

SOURCE UNKNOWN

Ostrich Stock

Makes 1.5 litres (2¾ pints)

1.5 kg (3¼ lb) ostrich neck
2.5 litres (4½ pints) water
2 stalks celery, coarsely chopped
2 large carrots, coarsely chopped
2 onions, coarsely chopped
5 ml (1 tsp) salt

Place all the ingredients in a large pot, bring to the boil and allow to simmer, uncovered, for 3–4 hours.

Strain through a fine sieve. The meat may be set aside for another dish that requires cooked ostrich meat. Discard the bones and vegetables.

Leave the stock to chill for 24 hours before it is used. The stock can also be stored in the freezer for future use.

PAULINE HENDERSON
MAGALIES OSTRICH RANCH, KROONDAL

Goulash Soup

Serves 8

500 g (1 lb 2 oz) cooked ostrich meat
(can be any cut)
115 g (4 oz) smoked ham
45 ml (3 tbsp) butter
45 ml (3 tbsp) oil
1 onion, diced
1 celery stalk, diced
1 red pepper, diced
45 ml (3 tbsp) flour
500 ml (2 cups) peeled, seeded and diced tomatoes
1.5 litres (2¾ pints) ostrich stock
(see recipe on the left)
5 ml (1 tsp) caraway seeds

Slice the ostrich and ham, then shred them.

Heat the butter and oil together in a large saucepan. Add the vegetables and sauté until tender. Sprinkle with flour and cook for 5 minutes or until the flour caramelizes.

Stir in the tomatoes and stock. Add the meat and simmer gently for 30–45 minutes. Sprinkle with caraway seeds and simmer for a further 5 minutes. Serve very hot.

SOURCE UNKNOWN

Ostrich Consommé with Savoury Custard Garnish

Serves 6

Custard Garnishes
2 eggs
4 egg yolks
250 ml (9 fl oz) ostrich stock
(see recipe on page 11)
a pinch each of salt, white pepper,
cayenne pepper and nutmeg
30 ml (2 tbsp) puréed carrot
30 ml (2 tbsp) puréed asparagus
30 ml (2 tbsp) tomato paste

Consommé
1.5 litres (2¾ pints) ostrich stock
(see recipe on page 11)

To make the garnishes, beat the eggs with the egg yolks. Add the stock and seasonings and divide equally between three bowls. Blend the carrot purée into the first bowl, asparagus purée into the second and tomato paste into the third. Pour the mixture into three small ovenproof dishes, place them in a large pan half filled with hot water and bake in a preheated oven at 180 °C (350 °F, Gas Mark 4) until very firm (20–25 minutes). Remove from the oven and, when cool, chill until completely set. Once set, cut into squares, diamonds, hearts or desired shape.

Heat the consommé, add the custard shapes, simmer for 5 minutes, then serve.

SOURCE UNKNOWN

Quick Ostrich Soup

Serves 6

45 ml (3 tbsp) oil
675 g (1½ lb) ostrich mince
1 large onion, chopped
2 cloves garlic, minced
875 ml (3½ cups) tinned, whole,
peeled tomatoes, undrained
1.5 litres (2¾ pints) water
6 beef stock cubes
(or 1.5 litres/2¾ pints ostrich stock, see page 11)
1 ml (¼ tsp) freshly ground black pepper
125 ml (½ cup) uncooked rice
375 ml (1½ cups) frozen peas,
carrots and corn vegetable blend
French bread (optional)

Heat the oil in a large saucepan and cook the mince, onion and garlic over medium heat until the meat browns. Stir to separate the mince.

Place the tomatoes, with juice, in a covered blender or food processor and process until smooth.

Add the tomatoes, water, stock cubes and pepper to the meat mixture. Bring to the boil over high heat, then reduce heat to low and simmer uncovered for 20 minutes.

Add the rice and vegetables and simmer for a further 15–20 minutes. Serve with French bread.

SOURCE UNKNOWN

French Onion and Ostrich Steak Soup

Serves 8

500 g (1 lb 2 oz) ostrich steak,
cut into very small pieces
60 ml (4 tbsp) flour
125 g (4½ oz) butter
1 large onion, chopped
30 ml (2 tbsp) salt
5 ml (1 tsp) white pepper
600 ml (1 pint) ostrich stock (see recipe on page 11),
or 4 bouillon cubes
750 g (1¾ lb) potatoes, cubed (optional)
5 large fresh brown mushrooms, sliced
250 ml (9 fl oz) red wine

Optional ingredients: 60 ml (4 tbsp) grated Cheddar cheese; 60 ml (4 tbsp) grated Mozzarella cheese; English muffins, split and toasted.

Coat the meat with the flour. Melt the butter in a soup pot and add the onion, meat and seasoning. Cook over medium heat until the onion is translucent and the liquid has darkened. Pour in the stock and stir. Add potatoes, mushrooms, wine and enough water to just cover the ingredients. Turn up the heat and stir until steam starts to appear. Reduce heat and simmer, covered, for about 30 minutes or until the potatoes are soft. Stir occasionally because the flour tends to stick to the bottom of the pot.

For a truly elegant and impressive presentation, half fill a heavy soup bowl with the soup, place half a toasted English muffin (split side up) on top, sprinkle some of the Cheddar and Mozzarella cheese on top of the muffin, place the bowls in a baking pan and put under the grill until the cheese has melted and started turning brown around the edges (about 5 minutes).

AMERICAN OSTRICH ASSOCIATION (SANDRA HILDRETH)

Minced Ostrich Chowder

Serves 6

150 g (5½ oz) ostrich mince
5 ml (1 tsp) soy sauce
2 ml (½ tsp) sugar
60 ml (4 tbsp) cornflour
30 ml (2 tbsp) oil
1–1.5 litres (1¾–2¾ pints) water
15 ml (1 tbsp) dry sherry
1 chicken stock cube
15 ml (1 tbsp) minced ginger
15 ml (1 tbsp) finely shredded spring onion
a few parsley sprigs, chopped
salt to taste
2 hard-boiled egg whites, grated

Place the meat in a bowl and add the soy sauce, sugar, 2 ml (½ tsp) cornflour, 15 ml (1 tbsp) oil and 30 ml (2 tbsp) water. Mix thoroughly and set the mince aside to marinate for 20 minutes.

Heat the remaining oil in a large saucepan. Sprinkle in the sherry, then add the crumbled stock cube and pour in all but 30 ml (2 tbsp) of the water. Bring to the boil, add the mince and simmer for 5 minutes.

Meanwhile, place the ginger, spring onion and half the parsley in a large soup bowl or divide between individual bowls. Blend the remaining cornflour to a smooth paste with the reserved water. Gradually pour this mixture into the simmering soup, stirring continuously to prevent lumps forming. Simmer for 1 minute.

Before serving, taste the soup and add seasoning if necessary. Stir in the egg whites and pour the soup into the prepared bowl(s). Garnish with the remaining parsley.

SOURCE UNKNOWN

STARTERS

Ostrich Liver Pâté

Serves 6

1 medium onion, chopped
4 cloves garlic, crushed
150 g (5½ oz) butter, cubed
200 g (7 oz) rindless pork belly, diced
100 g (3½ oz) streaky bacon, diced
700 g (1½ lb) ostrich liver, cubed
25 ml (5 tsp) brandy
5 ml (1 tsp) coriander seeds, cracked
20 ml (4 tsp) chopped parsley
5 ml (1 tsp) dried thyme
5 ml (1 tsp) prepared mustard
salt and freshly ground black pepper

In a pan, sauté the onion and garlic in a few cubes of butter until translucent. Add the pork belly and sauté slowly until cooked. Add the bacon, ostrich liver and brandy and continue to sauté until the liver is almost cooked. Remove from heat and allow to cool slightly.

Place the meat mixture and all remaining ingredients, except the butter, in a blender and process until smooth. Pour the mixture directly into small pâté bowls and smooth the surface. Melt the remaining butter and pour evenly over the surface of the pâté. Chill well.

Serve with lightly toasted whole-wheat bread or your favourite crackers.

KLEIN KAROO LANDBOU CO-OPERATIVE, CHEF QUENTIN SPICKERNELL

Ostrich Liver Pâté Roll-Ups

Serves 4

500 g (1 lb 2 oz) ostrich liver,
trimmed of membranes and fat, chopped
180 ml (6¼ fl oz) ostrich stock
(see recipe on page 11)
125 ml (4½ fl oz) white wine
60 ml (4 tbsp) finely chopped onion
1 ml (¼ tsp) ground ginger
15 ml (1 tbsp) light soy sauce
2 ml (½ tsp) Worcestershire sauce
1 ml (¼ tsp) each paprika, dried oregano,
dried thyme, white pepper and dried basil
2 ml (½ tsp) salt
125 g (4½ oz) butter, softened
15 ml (1 tbsp) brandy
8 crêpes (see recipe on page 126)

Cook the liver in the stock along with the wine, onion, ginger, soy sauce and Worcestershire sauce. Allow to cool completely, then strain and reserve the liquid.

Place the livers in a food processor and process with 30 ml (2 tbsp) of the reserved liquid. Add the seasonings, butter and brandy and process until light and smooth. Add more liquid if required to keep mixture soft. Spoon into a chilled bowl and refrigerate until ready to serve.

Just before serving, spread the mixture thickly over the crêpes, then roll them up in a Swiss-roll fashion. Slice the rolled crêpes into 2.5 cm (1 in) thick pieces, place on a tray, garnish with parsley and serve.

SOURCE UNKNOWN

Liver and Bacon en Croûte

Serves 6

500 g (1 lb 2 oz) ostrich liver,
trimmed of membranes and fat, coarsely chopped
45 ml (3 tbsp) butter
90 ml (6 tbsp) fresh breadcrumbs
2 hard-boiled eggs
1 small onion, coarsely chopped
10 ml (2 tsp) dried or 30 ml (2 tbsp)
chopped fresh parsley
5 ml (1 tsp) lemon juice
salt and freshly ground black pepper to taste
10 rashers rindless streaky bacon
10 croûtes

Fry the liver in heated butter until cooked. Place all the ingredients, except the bacon and croûtes, in a food processor or blender and chop coarsely.

Roll the bacon rashers tightly and secure with a cocktail stick. Grill under a preheated element until crisp. Spoon the liver mixture onto the croûtes and garnish with bacon rolls. Serve immediately.

SOURCE UNKNOWN

OTHER SERVING SUGGESTIONS

* The bacon may be fried until crisp, chopped and sprinkled over the liver.

* The liver mixture may be served as a snack with savoury biscuits or as a pâté in individual dishes.

Pickled Ostrich

Serves 8–12

1.5 kg (3 ¼ lb) ostrich buttock

Pickle
5 litres (8¾ pints) water
1.25 kg (2¾ lb) coarse salt
10 ml (2 tsp) potassium nitrate (saltpetre)
30 ml (2 tbsp) crushed coriander in muslin bag

First make the pickle by combining all the ingredients and boiling until the salt has dissolved. Leave to cool. Strain the pickle through muslin cloth into a wooden tub. Cut the ostrich buttock at the seams and place it in the pickle. Put the meat under weights and turn after 12 hours. Store in a cool place.

Replace the first pickled water with a second batch after 24 hours. Leave the meat in the pickle for 5 days. Rinse under running water, then cook in clean water until tender. Let it cool before serving as cold meat with salads.

SOURCE UNKNOWN

Ostrich Minestrone Milanese (page 10)

Ostrich Liver Pâté (page 15)

Ostrich Carpaccio

Serves 4

45 ml (3 tbsp) olive oil
30 ml (2 tbsp) fresh lemon juice
crushed garlic to taste
250 g (9 oz) ostrich fillet, very thinly sliced
salt and freshly ground black pepper

Mix together the olive oil, lemon juice and garlic in a dish. Lay the slices of fillet in the olive-oil mixture and dust with black pepper and salt. Stand for 2 hours. Serve on Melba toast or thinly sliced and toasted white bread.

SOURCE UNKNOWN

Ostrich and Cheese Dip

Serves 10

500 g (1 lb 2 oz) ostrich mince
125 ml (½ cup) chopped onion
750 g (1¾ lb) pre-sliced cheese
6 green chillies, chopped
15 ml (1 tbsp) Worcestershire sauce

Brown the meat and onion together, then add the remaining ingredients. Cook over low heat, stirring constantly, until the cheese has melted completely. Serve warm with your favourite crisps, cornchips or tortillas.

AMERICAN OSTRICH ASSOCIATION

Ostrich Appetizer Crescents

Makes 20 pieces

350 g (12 oz) ostrich mince
250 g (9 oz) cream cheese
90 ml (6 tbsp) grated Parmesan cheese
60 ml (4 tbsp) finely chopped onion
30 ml (2 tbsp) chopped parsley
15 ml (1 tbsp) milk
1 egg, beaten
5 ml (1 tsp) cold water
10 ready-made, uncooked dinner rolls
sesame and/or poppy seeds (optional)

Preheat the oven to 190 °C (375 °F, Gas Mark 4). Brown the mince, making sure the meat is crumbled. Combine the meat, cheeses, onion, parsley and milk. Mix until all ingredients are well blended. Combine the beaten egg with water and mix well. Cut each dinner roll in half. Place one spoonful of mixture to one side of the half, then fold the dough over the top of the mixture, pressing down to seal the edges. The rolls should now have semi-circle or crescent shape. Place on a greased baking sheet. Brush the tops with egg mixture, then sprinkle with sesame or poppy seeds. Bake for 10–15 minutes or until the dough turns a golden brown.

AMERICAN OSTRICH ASSOCIATION

Oriental Ostrich Meatballs in Sweet-and-Sour Sauce

Makes 30 meatballs

a pinch of garlic powder
1 ml (¼ tsp) salt
500 g ostrich mince
10 ml (2 tsp) oil
30 ml (2 tbsp) cornflour
1 x 410 g (14 oz) can crushed pineapple,
drained, juice reserved
1 green pepper, finely chopped
1 red or orange pepper, finely chopped
15 ml (1 tbsp) soy sauce
60 ml (4 tbsp) chopped cherries
15 ml (1 tbsp) sesame seeds
60 ml (4 tbsp) chopped onion
125 ml (½ cup) sugar
125 ml (4½ fl oz) white vinegar

Sprinkle garlic powder and salt over the mince and stir until evenly distributed. Shape the meat into about 30 small balls, then brown them in hot oil. Remove from the pan. Dissolve the cornflour in 125 ml (4½ fl oz) of the reserved pineapple juice. Place all remaining ingredients, except cornflour mixture, in a big pan or skillet, cover and cook over medium heat for 15 minutes. Add the cornflour mixture, increase heat and stir constantly until the mixture boils. Add the meatballs, then reduce heat and simmer for another 15 minutes. Serve hot.

AMERICAN OSTRICH ASSOCIATION

Ostrich and Creamed Spinach Phyllo Baskets

Serves 4

500 g (1 lb 2 oz) spinach
200 ml (7 fl oz) cream
20 ml (4 tsp) butter
1 large onion, finely chopped
150 g (5½ oz) bacon, cubed
250 g (9 oz) ostrich fillet, cut into strips
1 roll Phyllo pastry
1 egg, beaten

Wash and tear the spinach, then blanch for approximately 3 minutes in boiling water. Remove and rinse with cold water. Finely chop the spinach and sauté in a pot over low heat for 10 minutes. Add the cream and simmer over low heat until the liquid is reduced by half.

Melt the butter in a pan and sauté the onions until translucent. Add the bacon and fillet and fry until the fillet is medium done. Add the spinach and fry for 5 minutes.

Place the Phyllo sheets on a floured surface and cut into a dozen 12 x 12 cm (4¾ x 4¾ in) squares. Brush one square with egg, place another square on top of the first one, brush it with egg, then lay a third square on top. Place two tablespoons of the meat and spinach mixture in the middle of the pastry and fold the edges inwards to form a parcel. Brush the edges with egg. Repeat this with the remaining pastry until you have the required number of parcels.

Place the parcels on a greased baking tray and bake at 180 °C (350 °F, Gas Mark 4) for 15 minutes or until a golden brown.

CHEF THOMAS GROVE
GOBLINS COVE RESTAURANT, HEKPOORT

Cured Ostrich

Serves 4

500 g (1 lb 2 oz) ostrich fillet
sufficient red and white wine
(in equal amounts) to cover the fillet
750 g (1¾ lb) rock salt
100 g (3½ oz) sugar
10 bay leaves
3 cloves garlic, crushed
a large bunch of fresh rosemary
125 ml (½ cup) whole black peppercorns
8 moderately hot, dried chillies
peel of 1 orange

Place all the ingredients in a large bowl and leave covered and refrigerated for 7 days.

Remove the meat from the marinade and hang it in a cold room for approximately one week or until the meat feels firm.

Slice as thinly as possible, ideally on a slicer. Serve on a bed of salad leaves and sprinkle with extra-virgin olive oil and lemon juice.

THE AUSTRALIAN OSTRICH COMPANY

Ostrich Biltong Bites

Serves 8–10

1 loaf white bread
250 g (9 oz) soft butter
5 ml (1 tsp) lemon rind
250 ml (1 cup) grated ostrich biltong

Cut the bread into slices of 2 cm (¾ in) thick. Remove the crusts and cut the bread into 2 cm (¾ in) cubes (or divide each slice into nine cubes). Mix the butter and lemon rind and spread around each cube before rolling it in the grated biltong. Keep in a cool place until ready to serve.

DANELLE COULSON
HEKPOORT

Ostrich Bits

Makes 35 pieces

500 g (1 lb 2 oz) ostrich steak,
cut into 2 cm (¾ in) cubes
60 ml (4 tbsp) lemon juice
your favourite spices

Place all ingredients in a bowl, toss and refrigerate for at least 2 hours or overnight.

Arrange marinated meat in an ovenproof dish so that cubes are not touching each other and grill for 4 minutes.

May be served with or without a variety of steak sauces. Provide toothpicks.

FIONA BENSON
BLUE MOUNTAIN OSTRICH RANCH

Raw Ostrich with Mustard Dressing and Butter Lettuce

Serves 4

Mustard dressing
15 ml (1 tbsp) Dijon mustard
1 egg yolk
15 ml (1 tbsp) lemon juice
190 ml (6¾ fl oz) virgin olive oil
Worcestershire sauce
Tabasco sauce

4 x 60 g (2 oz) ostrich fillet
olive oil
butter lettuce
freshly ground black pepper
chopped chives
Parmesan cheese (optional)

For the mustard dressing, whisk together the mustard and egg yolk and add half the lemon juice. Slowly add the olive oil a little at a time, stirring until smoothly combined. Season with Worcestershire and Tabasco sauces, adding more lemon juice if necessary. Set aside.

Place the ostrich fillets between two sheets of wax paper brushed liberally with olive oil. Gently tap the meat with the flat side of a meat mallet until the slice is approximately 20 x 20 cm (8 x 8 in) and 2 mm (1/16 in) thick.

Arrange washed and dried lettuce leaves on the centre of four dinner plates. Gently remove one piece of wax paper from the ostrich slice and lay the slice on the lettuce leaves. Gently remove the other layer of wax paper, leaving the meat draped over the lettuce. Add the mustard dressing and garnish with freshly ground black pepper, chives and Parmesan cheese. Serve immediately.

THE AUSTRALIAN OSTRICH COMPANY

Ostrich Cho

Makes 25

500 g (1 lb 2 oz) ostrich steaks, thinly sliced
60 ml (4 tbsp) Oriental sweet-and-sour sauce

Preheat the oven to 180 °C (350 °F, Gas Mark 4). Spear the meat on the toothpicks so that it forms an accordion-style shape. Spoon the sauce over the meat. Place the skewered pieces in a greased baking dish and bake for 10 minutes.
  May be served hot or cold.

ORANGE GROVE OSTRICH FARM

Ostrich Hors d'oeuvre

Serves 4

Thinly slice 8 pieces of ostrich fillet and smoke them in a smoker until tender.
  Serve with grilled ostrich sausages, cantaloupe (spanspek) slices and a parsley garnish.

AMERICAN OSTRICH ASSOCIATION

Salads

Cold Ostrich Mould

Serves 12

20 ml (4 tsp) gelatine
375 ml (13 fl oz) ostrich stock
(see recipe on page 11), or
1 bouillon cube dissolved in 375 ml (13 fl oz) water
750 g (1¾ lb) ostrich tripe or salted ostrich biltong,
finely minced OR leftover ostrich mince
5 ml (1 tsp) grated lemon rind
5 ml (1 tsp) grated onion
salt and freshly ground black pepper to taste
500 ml (2 cups) cold minced ostrich meat
2 hard-boiled eggs, chopped
15 ml (1 tbsp) vinegar or 30 ml (2 tbsp) lemon juice
30 ml (2 tbsp) mayonnaise
125 ml (4½ fl oz) cream, beaten or
90 ml (6 tbsp) Ideal milk, chilled and beaten

Soak the gelatine in 300 ml (11 fl oz) stock. Place the tripe (or biltong), lemon rind, onion and remaining stock in a large saucepan and bring to the boil. Add in the gelatine and melt. Remove from heat. Mix in the cold ostrich, chopped egg and lemon juice. When the mixture starts to set, fold in the mayonnaise and beaten cream. Pour into a wet mould to set. Remove from mould and serve with a variety of salads.

KLEIN KAROO LANDBOU CO-OPERATIVE

Parisian Ostrich Salad

Serves 6–8

500 g (1 lb 2 oz) cooked ostrich meat
(any cut will do)
3 large potatoes, cooked and chopped
1 red onion, sliced
125 ml (4½ fl oz) olive oil
45 ml (3 tbsp) garlic vinegar
30 ml (2 tbsp) lemon juice
2 ml (½ tsp) each salt, pepper,
dried oregano and dried thyme
1 ml (¼ tsp) each dried basil,
garlic powder and onion powder
6–8 lettuce leaves
2 tomatoes, quartered
2 hard-boiled eggs, quartered

Cut the ostrich meat into small, bite-sized pieces and place in a bowl. Mix in the potatoes and onion. Blend the oil, vinegar, lemon and seasonings together and pour this over the meat and potato mixture. Marinate for 1 hour in the refrigerator.

Arrange lettuce leaves on a platter and tip the salad on top of the leaves. Garnish with tomato and egg. Serve very cold.

SOURCE UNKNOWN

Potato and Biltong Salad

Serves 6

8 large potatoes
15 ml (1 tbsp) olive oil
30 ml (2 tbsp) vinegar
3 spring onions, chopped
5 radishes, diced
2 stalks celery, diced
250 ml (9 fl oz) mayonnaise
15 ml (1 tbsp) prepared mustard
3 hard-boiled eggs, chopped
5 ml (1 tsp) salt
2 ml (½ tsp) white pepper
115 g (4 oz) ostrich biltong, finely sliced

Peel and dice the potatoes. Place in a pot with salted water and boil until soft. Drain and rinse under cold water to cool.

Place the potatoes in a large bowl and sprinkle with oil and vinegar. Stir in the onions, radishes and celery.

In a small mixing bowl, blend the mayonnaise, mustard, eggs, salt and pepper. Fold into the potatoes together with the biltong.

SOURCE UNKNOWN

Ostrich and Pasta Salad

Serves 6

500 g (1 lb 2 oz) ostrich meat (any cut will do), cooked and diced
3 tomatoes, peeled, seeded and chopped
1 carrot, finely diced
1 red pepper, finely chopped
1 green pepper, finely chopped
3 spring onions, chopped
1 litre (4 cups) chilled, cooked pasta*
125 ml (4½ fl oz) mayonnaise
45 ml (3 tbsp) chilli sauce
15 ml (1 tbsp) lemon juice
2 ml (½ tsp) each onion powder and garlic powder
5 ml (1 tsp) chilli powder
3 drops Tabasco sauce
6 large curly lettuce leaves
parsley tufts

Mix the ostrich, vegetables and pasta together in a large mixing bowl.

In a separate bowl, blend the mayonnaise, chilli sauce, lemon juice, seasoning and Tabasco, pour over the salad and toss.

Place the lettuce leaves on chilled plates, top with salad, garnish with parsley and serve.

SOURCE UNKNOWN

* A GOOD PASTA TO USE WITH THIS DISH IS ORZO — A SMALL RICE-SHAPED PASTA.

Warm Ostrich Salad

Serves 2

100 g (3 ½ oz) assorted salad leaves
1 cucumber, thinly sliced
8 cherry tomatoes, quartered
1 punnet fresh raspberries
250 ml (9 fl oz) red-wine vinegar
30 ml (2 tbsp) castor sugar
40 g (1 ½ oz) ostrich fillet, cut into strips
olive oil
butter
salt and freshly ground black pepper

Arrange the salad leaves, cucumber and cherry tomatoes on each plate. Place the vinegar, raspberries and castor sugar in a saucepan, bring to the boil, then reduce heat and simmer. Fry the ostrich strips in olive oil and butter, season, then place them on top of the salad leaves. Blend the warm dressing and then dress the salad.
Garnish as desired.

CHEF CRAIG GRAVETT
SA CHEF'S ASSOCIATION

Ostrich Steak Salad

Serves 4

1 brinjal
virgin olive oil
1 baby marrow
4 Roma tomatoes
salt and freshly ground black pepper
balsamic vinegar
200 g (7 oz) ostrich steak,
cut approximately 3 mm (⅛ in) thick
fresh basil

Slice and salt the brinjal and stand for 15 minutes before rinsing. Brush with olive oil and char-grill. Cut the baby marrow into 1 cm (⅜ in) thick slices, brush with olive oil and char-grill. Halve the tomatoes lengthways, season and place under a hot grill for 4–5 minutes or until they are soft and browned. Place all the vegetables in a wide bowl and dress with 1 part vinegar to 4 parts oil.

Brush the steak with olive oil and season. Place on a preheated charcoal grill and cook to the desired degree – medium-rare is recommended.

Allow steaks to rest for 10 minutes in a warm place. Place the warm vegetable salad on a serving plate, garnish with fresh basil and top with ostrich steaks.

SOURCE UNKNOWN

Ostrich Herb Salad

Serves 6

mixed herbs
250 g (9 oz) ostrich steak, thinly sliced
1 onion, chopped
1 green pepper, chopped
1 lettuce, shredded
tortilla chips
250 ml (1 cup) shredded red cabbage
2 tomatoes, diced
250 ml (1 cup) grated Cheddar cheese
2 avocados, diced
sour cream
salsa

Sprinkle the herbs over the meat, grill together with the onion and green pepper until tender (4–5 minutes).

Cover four plates with lettuce and arrange the tortilla chips around the edge of the plates. Top the lettuce with cabbage, then tomatoes and then the grilled onion and green pepper. Arrange the meat on top and sprinkle with cheese and avocado.

Serve with sour cream and salsa.

AMERICAN OSTRICH ASSOCIATION

Cured Ostrich Salad

Serves 8

1 ostrich fillet
sufficient red and white wine
(in equal amounts) to cover the meat
750 g (1¾ lb) rock salt
100 g (3½ oz) sugar
10 bay leaves
3 cloves garlic, crushed
a large bunch of fresh rosemary
125 ml (½ cup) whole black peppercorns
8 dried chillies
peel of 1 orange

Place all the ingredients in a large bowl and leave covered and refrigerated for 7 days.

Remove meat from the marinade and hang it in a cold room for about one week or until the meat feels firm.

Slice as thinly as possible, ideally on a slicer. Serve with extra-virgin olive oil, salad leaves and lemon juice.

AMERICAN OSTRICH ASSOCIATION

Ostrich and Avocado Salad

Serves 4

500 g (1 lb 2 oz) ostrich fillet
30 ml (2 tbsp) butter
250 g (9 oz) shrimps or prawns, peeled,
de-veined and boiled
15 ml (1 tbsp) parsley flakes
5 ml (1 tsp) grated Parmesan cheese
2 ml (½ tsp) mixed spices
lettuce
1 avocado, peeled, pitted and sliced
3 fresh pears, pared and sliced
(apples may also be used)
poppy-seed dressing or choice of dressing

Slightly flatten the fillet between two sheets of wax paper using a wooden or rubber mallet, and cut it into 2.5 cm (1 in) thick slices.

Melt the butter in a skillet, and add the ostrich, shrimps, parsley, cheese and spices. Sauté until the meat and shrimps are cooked. Drain on paper towel and blot any excess butter. Place in the refrigerator to cool.

Arrange lettuce leaves on individual salad plates. Place meat, shrimp, avocado slices and pear slices on top of the lettuce. Drizzle on dressing and serve cold.

PAULINE HENDERSON
MAGALIES OSTRICH RANCH, KROONDAL

Ostrich Fillet Salad

Serves 4

1 hard-boiled egg
5 ml (1 tsp) finely chopped parsley
500 g (1 lb 2 oz) ostrich fillet, diced
100 g (3½ oz) streaky bacon,
blanched and finely shredded
salt and freshly ground black pepper to taste
400 ml (14 fl oz) ostrich stock
(see recipe on page 11), or beef stock
7.5 g (¼ oz) gelatine powder
lettuce hearts and watercress to garnish

Preheat the oven to 160 °C (325 °F, Gas Mark 3).

Peel and slice the egg and decorate the bottom of a baking tin (about 15 cm/6 in diameter) with the slices of egg and chopped parsley.

Mix the ostrich and bacon, season and add any remaining pieces of egg. Add 250 ml (9 fl oz) stock and mix in thoroughly. Spoon the mixture into the tin, cover with foil and bake for 1½–2 hours.

Dissolve the gelatine in the remaining stock, season well and strain this liquid into the tin. When cold and set, turn out the mould onto a serving platter and garnish with lettuce and watercress.

SOURCE UNKNOWN

Ostrich Fillet and Green Pepper Salad

Serves 4

1 thick slice (about 250 g/9 oz) ostrich fillet
15 ml (1 tbsp) olive oil
1 shallot or spring onion, finely chopped
5 ml (1 tsp) tomato purée
60 ml (4 tbsp) sherry
100 g (3½ oz) button mushrooms
100 g (3½ oz) cooked ham
2 green peppers, sliced
French dressing
225 g (8 oz) tomatoes, sliced

Sauté the fillet in oil until golden brown on each side. Add the shallot and continue cooking for 2–3 minutes. Stir in the tomato purée, add the sherry and cover and simmer for 5 minutes. Add the whole mushrooms and cook for a further 5 minutes. Leave to cool.

Cut the ham into shreds. Slice, blanch and refresh the peppers. Cut the fillet into thick julienne strips and then mix all the ingredients, except the tomato slices, with the French dressing. Place on a serving dish and garnish with tomato slices.

SOURCE UNKNOWN

Ostrich Salad

Serves 6

250 g (9 oz) cold, cooked ostrich fillet
(preferably underdone)
5 ml (1 tsp) paprika
2 ml (½ tsp) mustard powder
freshly ground black pepper to taste
½ clove garlic crushed with 2 ml (½ tsp) salt
15 ml (1 tbsp) red-wine vinegar
45 ml (3 tbsp) oil
1 dill cucumber
12 black olives
250 g (9 oz) tomatoes
6 slices of French bread

Cut the fillet into slices of 12 mm (½ in) thick and then into thin strips. Mix the seasonings and garlic with the vinegar and whisk in the oil. When thick, pour the mixture over the fillet strips and leave to marinate while preparing the other ingredients.

Slice the cucumber, halve and stone the olives and scald, skin and quarter the tomatoes. Scoop out the seeds.

Arrange the bread slices in a serving dish and place a large spoonful of the fillet and dressing on each slice. Arrange the sliced cucumber between every other portion of meat, with the olives on top, and fill in the gaps with the quartered tomatoes.

SOURCE UNKNOWN

Main Courses

Fillet & Steak

Peppered Fillet with Peppers and Hummus

Serves 6

6 peppers, assorted colours
olive oil
salt and freshly ground black pepper
125 ml (½ cup) peppercorns
500 g (1 lb 2 oz) whole ostrich fillet
⅓ loaf white bread, crust removed
25 ml (5 tsp) olive oil
2 sprigs rosemary
25 ml (5 tsp) coarse salt
200 g (7 oz) hummus
1 x 110 g (4 oz) tin anchovies

Dressing
60 ml (4 tbsp) olive oil
45 ml (3 tbsp) Balsamic vinegar
30 ml (2 tbsp) capers, chopped
20 ml (4 tsp) grated Parmesan cheese
salt and freshly ground black pepper
2 ml (½ tsp) dried marjoram

Halve the peppers lengthways, place on a hot tray, flesh side down, and position under a hot pre-heated grill until the skins begin to blister and char slightly. Remove and allow to cool. Peel off the outer membranes and remove the inner seed pulp, slice thickly and season with salt, pepper and olive oil. Set aside.

Crack the peppercorns on a hard surface with the base of a heavy pan. Once coarsely cracked, spread evenly on a board and press the fillet into the corns to create an even crust. Repeat on the opposite side.

In a well-heated pan, sear both sides of the fillet, then set aside to cool.

Break off thumb-sized chunks of bread and toss in oil, rosemary and coarse salt until liberally coated. Place on a flat tray and toast evenly under a moderate grill.

Thinly slice the fillet and stack in roughly defined layers, alternating between the fillet, peppers, hummus, anchovies and croutons.

Combine the dressing ingredients in a jar and shake well. Dress and serve immediately.

KLEIN KAROO LANDBOU CO-OPERATIVE, CHEF QUENTIN SPICKERNELL

Ostrich Fillet in Naartjie Sauce (page 36)

Ostrich and Avocado Salad (page 28)

Stuffed Ostrich Fillet

Serves 2

assorted vegetables of your choice
200 g (7 oz) de-veined spinach
diced onions
30 g (1 oz) pistachio nuts
butter
120 g (4 oz) Chinese noodles
2 x 220 g (7¾ oz) thick ostrich fillets
100 ml (3½ fl oz) sherry
ostrich stock (see recipe on page 11)

Blanch and refresh the vegetables and spinach. Sauté the spinach, onions and pistachio nuts in butter.

Blanch the Chinese noodles and refresh.

Make a hole lengthways through the centre of each fillet, then stuff with the spinach mixture. Seal the fillet in a hot pan, then place it in the oven for 15 minutes at 200 °C (400 °F, Gas Mark 6).

Deglaze the pan with sherry, then add stock and reduce. Reheat the noodles. Sauté the vegetables. Place the noodles in the centre of a platter and arrange the vegetables around the border. Slice each fillet in five pieces and fan it around the noodles. Drizzle the sauce over the fillet and garnish as desired. Serve immediately.

CHEF CRAIG GRAVETT
SA CHEF'S ASSOCIATION

Smoked Ostrich with Lenrolto

Serves 2

100 ml (3½ fl oz) sunflower oil
20 ml (4 tsp) olive oil
4 cloves garlic, chopped
2 onions, finely chopped
2 carrots, finely chopped
2 leeks, finely chopped
20 ml (4 tsp) each dried coriander,
dried basil and dried parsley
4 sticks fennel, finely chopped
500 g (1 lb 2 oz) green lentils, soaked for 24 hours
1.5 litres (2¾ pints) ostrich stock
(see recipe on page 11)
salt and freshly ground black pepper
160 g (5½ oz) Parmesan cheese, grated
500 g (1 lb 2 oz) smoked ostrich fillet, thinly sliced
cornflour
8 tomatoes, peeled and diced

Heat oils over moderate heat. Add the garlic, then all the vegetables and sweat for a few minutes. Add half the herbs. Add the drained lentils and cook for 1 minute. Add 1 litre (1¾ pints) ostrich stock and season. Simmer until cooked and the liquid has evaporated. Add the Parmesan cheese and check seasoning.

Arrange the lentils and smoked ostrich on a serving platter. Thicken remaining stock with cornflour and add remaining herbs and diced tomatoes. Pour the sauce over the ostrich and lentils. Serve warm.

CHEF MARK CHARLISH
SA CHEF'S ASSOCIATION

Ostrich Medallions with Kahlúa Cream Sauce

Serves 4

4 medium or 8 small carrots
125 ml (½ cup) mange tout (snow peas)
4 yellow patty pans
1 onion, diced
120 g (4 oz) button mushrooms, sliced
50 g (1¾ oz) sliced leeks
500 ml (18 fl oz) fresh cream
salt and freshly ground black pepper
4 potatoes
200 g (7 oz) clarified butter
8 x 120 g (4 oz) ostrich fillet medallions
olive oil
butter
80 ml (2¾ fl oz) white wine
120 ml (4¼ fl oz) Kahlúa
80 g (2¾ oz) gooseberries

Prepare, blanch and refresh the carrots, mange tout and patty pans.

Sauté the onions, mushrooms and leeks, add half the cream and season to taste. Simmer over low heat for about 15 minutes.

Peel, grate and season the potatoes, then fry in clarified butter until the edges turn brown. Turn the potato and brown the other side. Remove from the pan and place on a paper towel to drain excess oil.

Seal the ostrich medallions in olive oil and butter, then remove from the pan and set aside.

To make the sauce, deglaze the pan with white wine. Add Kahlúa, gooseberries and remaining cream, and reduce. Season to taste.

Reheat the meat and potato. Sauté the vegetables in olive oil or microwave. Arrange some potato in the centre of each plate. Place one medallion on top, top with the onion, mushroom and leek mixture, then place a second medallion on top of this. Repeat for each plate. Sprinkle vegetables around the edge of the plate and pour sauce over the top to cover the medallions. Garnish as desired. Serve immediately.

CHEF CRAIG GRAVETT
SA CHEF'S ASSOCIATION

Stuffed Ostrich Fillet with Cheese Sauce

Serves 6

2 kg (4½ lb) ostrich fillet
salt, pepper and nutmeg to taste
10 ml (2 tsp) gelatine

Filling
3 medium onions, sliced
300 g (11 oz) button mushrooms, sliced
45 ml (3 tbsp) butter
1 x 410 g (14 oz) can pineapple pieces,
drained and finely chopped
5 ml (1 tsp) garlic flakes
250 ml (1 cup) rice, cooked
½ chicken stock cube, crumbled
beef tongue, cooked and finely minced

Sauce
60 ml (4 tbsp) butter
60 ml (4 tbsp) flour
250 ml (9 fl oz) milk, heated
140 ml (5 fl oz) ostrich stock,
reserved from cooked fillet
125 ml (4½ fl oz) dry white wine
5 ml (1 tsp) prepared mustard
salt to taste
1 ml (¼ tsp) black pepper
300 ml (1¼ cup) grated Cheddar cheese
125 ml (4½ fl oz) cream

Season the fillet with salt, pepper and nutmeg and sprinkle with gelatine.

Fry the onions and mushrooms in butter, add remaining filling ingredients and mix well.

Slit the fillet to form a pouch and stuff with filling. Secure the opening with toothpicks and tie it up into a parcel with string. Wrap the fillet in aluminium foil and bake in a preheated oven at 180 °C (350 °F, Gas Mark 4) for approximately 2 hours or until cooked. Remove the fillet from the foil, reserving stock, and place it in a heated roasting pan while preparing the sauce.

To prepare the sauce, melt the butter, then stir in the flour and add the milk, reserved stock and wine. Stir over low heat until thick and smooth. Add seasonings, cheese and cream and stir until smooth.

Pour the sauce over the fillet and return to the oven for 20 minutes.

ORIENT BUTCHERY
MAGALIESBURG

Ostrich Fillet Steak

Serves 4

10 ml (2 tsp) olive oil
4 x 250 g (9 oz) ostrich fillet steaks
salt and freshly ground black pepper
60 ml (4 tbsp) Baines Prickly Pear liqueur
15 ml (1 tbsp) green peppercorns, bruised
250 ml (9 fl oz) cream
juice of 1 lemon

Heat a heavy cast-iron pan, preferably with grooves, until very hot. Brush with oil and fry the steaks for approximately 2 minutes on each side, depending on thickness. Remove and place on a warmed serving plate. Season with salt and pepper.

Heat the remaining ingredients, except the lemon juice, in a small pan. Season and cook to reduce to a good consistency. Add lemon juice to taste and pour the sauce over the fillets. Serve immediately.

SOURCE UNKNOWN

Ostrich Fillet in Naartjie Sauce

Serves 4–6

500 g (1 lb 2 oz) ostrich fillet*
5–7 ml (1–1½ tsp) beef stock powder
juice and grated peel of 1 large orange
60 ml (4 tbsp) medium-cream sherry
15 ml (1 tbsp) honey
freshly ground black pepper
30 ml (2 tbsp) olive oil
2 naartjies, peeled and segmented (or in a can)

Rub the ostrich with beef stock powder and place in a shallow dish. Mix the orange juice and peel, sherry, honey and black pepper. Pour over the fillet and marinate for at least 1 hour. Preheat oven to 200 °C (400 °F, Gas Mark 6).

Pour olive oil into a roasting pan and heat for a minute or two. Remove fillet from marinade and place in hot oil. Roast for about 5 minutes. Brush with marinade. Add the naartjie segments and roast for a further 10 minutes or until cooked.

FAIR LADY, 16 OCTOBER 1996

* OSTRICH STEAK MAY BE USED INSTEAD OF FILLET, BUT THEN PAN-FRY OR GRILL THE MEAT INSTEAD OF ROASTING IT.

Ostrich Steak with Green Peppercorn and Sultana Sauce

Serves 4

Sauce
45 ml (3 tbsp) butter
2 onions, sliced
1 clove garlic, crushed
30 ml (2 tbsp) flour
200 ml (7 fl oz) beef stock
45 ml (3 tbsp) port
45 ml (3 tbsp) sultanas, soaked in warm water
10 ml (2 tsp) green peppercorns
10 ml (2 tsp) Dijon mustard
100 ml (3½ fl oz) cream
salt and freshly ground black pepper to taste

4 ostrich fillet steaks
30 ml (2 tbsp) oil
30 ml (2 tbsp) butter

To prepare the sauce, melt the butter in a saucepan and sauté the onions and garlic until soft. Stir in the flour and cook for 1 minute. Add the stock and port gradually, stirring constantly. Cook until the sauce has thickened, then add the sultanas, peppercorns, mustard, cream and seasoning. Cook over low heat for 1 minute, then remove from heat, cover and set aside.

To prepare the steaks, heat the butter and oil together in a large, heavy-based frying pan. Fry the steaks over high heat for 2–3 minutes on each side. Serve immediately, accompanied by the sauce.

JOEY GOOSEN
RUSTENBURG

Ostrich Steak with Peppercorn Wine Sauce

Serves 4

500 g (1 lb 2 oz) ostrich steaks
7 ml (1½ tsp) cornflour
250 ml (9 fl oz) beef stock
1 ml (¼ tsp) dried thyme
1 small bay leaf
30 ml (2 tbsp) red wine
1 ml (¼ tsp) black peppercorns, crushed

Heat a large, heavy skillet over medium heat for 5 minutes. Place the steaks in the skillet for 2–3 minutes, turning once, until the juices run clear.

While the steaks are cooking, in small pan dissolve the cornflour in the stock. Bring to the boil and cook until slightly thickened (about 1 minute). Stir in the thyme and bay leaf. Lower heat and cook until the liquid is reduced by half. Stir in the wine and peppercorns. Cook for about 3 minutes, stirring occasionally. Remove bay leaf.

Place the steaks on individual serving plates and spoon over the sauce.

AMERICAN OSTRICH ASSOCIATION

Pan-seared Ostrich

Serves 4

45 ml (3 tbsp) butter or oil
coarsely ground black pepper
salt
4 x 200 g (7 oz) ostrich steaks or fillet
5 ml (1 tsp) jerepigo or muscadel wine
juice of 1 lemon

Heat the butter or oil in a heavy-based saucepan. Season the steaks with salt and pepper and quickly sear on both sides, then add the wine and lemon juice, coating each steak well. Cook an additional 3 minutes on each side. The steaks are ready when the outside is dark brown and the inside is pink.

CHRIS PATON
PRETORIA

Pan-fried Ostrich Fillet

Serves 6

1.5 kg (3¼ lb) ostrich fillet, thickly sliced
350 g (12 oz) pork fat
15 ml (1 tbsp) salt
2 ml (½ tsp) black pepper
2 ml (½ tsp) dried thyme
2 ml (½ tsp) oil
15 ml (1 tbsp) sugar
125 ml (4½ fl oz) tomato sauce
125 ml (4½ fl oz) meat extract (1 bouillon cube)
125 ml (4½ fl oz) vinegar, lemon juice or wine
15 ml (1 tbsp) Worcestershire sauce
1 onion, finely chopped

Make incisions in the meat and stuff with pork fat.
Mix all remaining ingredients and marinate the meat for 2–3 days in the refrigerator. Turn 3 times a day.
In a heavy-based pan, cook the meat in a little oil until tender, basting regularly with the marinade. Slice and serve hot or cold.

KLEIN KAROO LANDBOU CO-OPERATIVE

Mock Duck

Serves 4

500 g (1 lb 2 oz) ostrich steak,
12–20 mm (½–¾ in) thick
15 ml (1 tbsp) cracked black pepper
15 ml (1 tbsp) salt
1 ml (¼ tsp) dried parsley

Stuffing
625 ml (2½ cups) toasted breadcrumbs
½ onion, chopped
5 ml (1 tsp) dried thyme
5 ml (1 tsp) dried sage
60 ml (4 tbsp) crushed, toasted almonds
1 clove garlic, crushed
125 ml (½ cup) melted butter
30 ml (2 tbsp) Worcestershire sauce
boiling water

Orange sauce
125 ml (½ cup) orange marmalade
250 ml (9 fl oz) fresh orange juice

Garnish
red maraschino cherries
thin orange slices
parsley sprigs

To prepare the meat, cut it in half, then slice through the middle, almost but not quite through to the other side, making a pita-style pocket. Combine the pepper, salt and parsley and rub into both sides of the steak.

Combine all the dry stuffing ingredients, then add the melted butter, Worcestershire sauce and enough boiling water to moisten well. Stand for 20 minutes to allow the bread crumbs to absorb the liquid. Stir well. Stuff each half of the steak, roll and fasten with skewers.

Combine the marmalade and orange juice, mixing well. Bake for 2 hours at 160 °C (325 °F, Gas Mark 3), basting every 30 minutes with the orange sauce.

Remove from the oven, slice the meat and arrange it on a serving platter. Cover the slices with the remaining orange sauce and garnish with cherries, orange slices and parsley sprigs.

AMERICAN OSTRICH ASSOCIATION

Seared Ostrich set on Toasted Sunflower Polenta with Flash-fried Vegetables and Tapenade Sauce

Serves 10

Meat dish
40 g (1½ oz) chopped marjoram
20 g (¾ oz) crushed black pepper
200 ml (7 fl oz) balsamic vinegar
150 ml (5¼ fl oz) ketjap manis
(Indonesian sweet soy sauce)
1.5 kg (3¼ lb) ostrich fillet

Polenta cake
15 ml (1 tbsp) olive oil
10 ml (2 tsp) chopped onions
5 ml (1 tsp) chopped garlic
150 g (5½ oz) sunflower seeds, toasted
200 g (7 oz) polenta
200 ml (7 fl oz) chicken stock
salt and freshly ground black pepper
10 ml (2 tsp) grated Parmesan cheese

Vegetables
300 g (11 oz) oyster mushrooms, chopped
200 g (7 oz) mange tout (snow peas), chopped
5 plum tomatoes, halved
45 ml (3 tbsp) olive oil
10 ml (2 tsp) each dried basil,
dried thyme and dried parsley
10 ml (2 tsp) rock salt
5 ml (1 tsp) crushed black pepper

Red pepper pesto
100 g (3½ oz) whole red peppers
100 g (3½ oz) garlic cloves, peeled and crushed
10 ml (2 tsp) roasted chilli
10 ml (2 tsp) roasted almonds
10 ml (2 tsp) olive oil
20 ml (4 tsp) white-wine vinegar
20 g (¾ oz) grated Parmesan cheese
salt and freshly ground black pepper

Tapenade sauce
100 ml (3½ fl oz) chicken stock
500 ml (18 fl oz) meat stock
50 g (1¾ oz) black olive paste
8 g (¼ oz) anchovy fillets
10 ml (2 tsp) olive oil
100 g (3½ oz) butter
salt and freshly ground black pepper

Mix the marjoram, pepper, balsamic vinegar and ketjap manis and marinate the ostrich in it for at least 4 hours.

To make the polenta cake, add olive oil to a pot and sauté the onions, garlic and sunflower seeds. Add the polenta and cook together for a few minutes. Add the chicken stock and cook for about 1 hour. Remove from heat, then add the seasoning and cheese. Leave to cool.

Prepare the mushrooms and mange tout and set aside. Season the tomatoes and sprinkle with olive oil and half of the herbs. Slow roast the tomatoes for about 2 hours at 100 °C (200 °F, Gas Mark ¼) – the longer they roast, the more intense the flavour.

For the pesto, grill the whole peppers in a hot oven for 10 minutes. De-seed, skin and blend in a food processor, together with the garlic, chilli, almonds, olive oil, vinegar and cheese. Season to taste.

To make the tapenade sauce, heat the chicken and meat stock until it reduces to a thicker consistency – if necessary, thicken with beurre manié (15 ml/1 tbsp butter and 15 ml/1 tbsp flour mixture). Add olive paste and chopped anchovies and slowly blend in the olive oil and butter, preferably with an electric blender. Season to taste.

After the pesto and sauce have been prepared, shape the cold polenta mixture into flat teardrop shapes. Sprinkle with olive oil and place on a baking tray for reheating.

Seal the meat in a hot pan and proceed as follows: roast the marinated and seasoned meat at 220 °C (425 °F, Gas Mark 6) for approximately 20 minutes until medium done. Remove and set aside to rest (for the tissue to relax after the cooking process and to filter out any remaining blood).

Place the mushrooms and mange tout in a hot skillet and flash-fry them in olive oil. Season with rock salt and pepper. Add the remaining herbs. Remove the tomatoes from the oven and set aside.

Arrange warmed polenta cake on each plate and top with a tomato. Spoon the vegetable mixture on the side and arrange the thinly sliced fillet on top of the vegetables. Lastly, place a dollop of pesto on the fillet slices and garnish the plate with tapenade sauce.

THIS DISH WAS PREPARED BY THE SOUTH AFRICAN RAPS TEAM AT THE INTERNATIONAL COMPETITION HELD IN LUXEMBOURG IN NOVEMBER 1997. THANKS TO CHRIS VAN WYK, FANCOURT HOTEL, GEORGE.

Ostrich Wellington

Serves 6–8

1 kg (2¼ lb) ostrich fillet
pepper
butter
100 g (3½ oz) button mushrooms
15 ml (1 tbsp) dried mixed herbs and parsley
1 roll puff pastry
1 egg (for glazing)
parsley to garnish

Trim and tie up the fillet with string and dust it with pepper. Heat the butter in a frying pan and quickly brown the meat all over. Roast the meat at 220 °C (425 °F, Gas Mark 6) for 10 minutes. Leave to cool, then remove string.

In the meantime, slice the mushrooms and sauté them in butter for a few minutes. Remove from heat and add herbs and parsley. Leave to cool.

Roll out the puff pastry into a rectangular shape. Divide it in two, making one piece two-thirds larger than the other. Spoon the mushroom mixture onto the larger piece. Lay the meat on top and fold up and press the pastry around it. Lay the smaller piece of pastry over the top and press the edges together. Brush with egg glaze and decorate if desired. Bake at 220 °C (425 °F, Gas Mark 6) for 35–40 minutes or until well browned.

Serve immediately.

SOURCE UNKNOWN

Pressed Pepper Ostrich Fillet

Serves 4

15 ml (1 tbsp) oil
1 kg (2¼ lb) ostrich fillet
15 ml (1 tbsp) prepared English mustard
50 g (1¾ oz) black peppercorns, coarsely crushed

Heat the oil in a frying pan and fry the meat quickly on all sides to seal it. This should take no longer than 2 minutes.

Smear the mustard over the ostrich and roll it in the crushed peppercorns, pressing down firmly so that they adhere. Wrap it tightly in foil and chill for at least 2 hours.

Place the fillet, still in its foil, in a roasting pan and cook at 230 °C (450 °F, Gas Mark 6) for 25 minutes.

Transfer the fillet to a board and loosen the foil, taking care not to disturb the pepper crust. Put another board on top, apply 1–2 kg (2¼–4½ lb) of weight (about several large, full tins) and leave it in the refrigerator overnight.

Serve cold and cut into very thin slices. The combination of chilled, rare meat and fiery but aromatic peppercorns is simply sensational. If desired, the peppercorns can be scraped off just before serving – their fragrance will have permeated the meat.

SOURCE UNKNOWN

Asian Ostrich Medallions
and Stir-fried Greens

Serves 4

500 g (1 lb 2 oz) ostrich fillet
15 ml (1 tbsp) coarse black pepper
light sesame-seed oil
1 spring onion
250 ml (9 fl oz) dry red wine
250 ml (9 fl oz) ostrich stock (or beef)
dried red chilli flakes to taste
1 clove garlic, chopped
1 x 2 cm (¾ in) piece fresh ginger, chopped
60 ml (4 tbsp) unsalted butter
30 ml (2 tbsp) fresh coriander, chopped
15 ml (1 tbsp) dark soy sauce

Vegetables

20 ml (4 tsp) light sesame-seed oil
125 ml (½ cup) bean shoots
125 ml (½ cup) mange tout (snow peas)
250 ml (1 cup) leafy green Chinese cabbage
125 ml (½ cup) Chinese mushrooms

Rub the ostrich with pepper and oil and set aside. Place the onion and wine in a saucepan and reduce by two-thirds. Add stock, chilli flakes, garlic and ginger. Reduce until the sauce begins to thicken slightly.

Whisk in the butter away from the heat and add the coriander and soy sauce. Keep warm.

Heat a heavy-based pan, add the ostrich and cook until medium rare. Set aside to rest.

Heat the sesame oil and add the vegetables. Toss over high heat for approximately 2–3 minutes. Spoon the vegetables on the centre of a plate or platter, top with sliced ostrich and finish with the sauce.

THE AUSTRALIAN OSTRICH COMPANY

Fillet of Ostrich Stuffed with Smoked Oyster Pâté and Served with Smoked Oyster Sauce

Serves 4

Pâté
1 x 110 g (4 oz) tin smoked oysters, drained
25 ml (5 tsp) cream cheese
25 ml (5 tsp) fruit chutney

Sauce
45 ml (3 tbsp) butter
150 g (5½ oz) flour
150 ml (5¼ fl oz) milk, warmed
2 x 110 g (4 oz) tins smoked oysters
salt and freshly ground black pepper to taste

500 g (1 lb 2 oz) ostrich fillet

To make the pâté, blend all ingredients together in a food processor until smooth.

To make the sauce, melt the butter and add the flour, stirring to a smooth paste. Gradually add the warmed milk, whisking all the time. Bring to the boil and add the smoked oysters and seasoning. Simmer over low heat until the sauce is cooked.

Preheat the oven to 220 °C (425 °F, Gas Mark 6), wrap the fillet in tin foil and roast for 25 minutes (medium-rare). Remove meat from the foil, make a thin slice the length of the fillet and stuff with pâté. To seal, grill the side with the stuffing.

Serve with the oyster sauce and basmati rice.

CHEF THOMAS GROVE

GOBLINS COVE RESTAURANT, HEKPOORT

Ostrich and Prawns in Roasted Garlic Sauce

Serves 4

12 pieces ostrich fillet, sliced medallion size and pounded into scaloppini
15–20 medium-sized garlic cloves, peeled
90 ml (6 tbsp) butter
1 medium-sized red onion, finely chopped
375 ml (13 fl oz) dry white wine (preferably Chardonnay)
750 ml (1¼ pints) heavy whipping cream
salt and freshly ground black pepper to taste
15 ml (1 tbsp) olive oil
8 large prawns
125 ml (4½ fl oz) ostrich stock (see recipe on page 11)

Prepare the ostrich and set aside.

Place the garlic cloves in a roasting pan and bake at 200 °C (400 °F, Gas Mark 6) until soft and brown (about 10–15 minutes). Melt the butter in a saucepan and sauté the onion until it is fully cooked (about 5 minutes). Add wine and allow to cook over medium heat. When liquid is reduced by half, add the roasted garlic and purée the mixture. Place back on medium heat and slowly add the cream, salt and pepper. Bring to the boil and set aside.

In a separate pan, heat the olive oil, add the ostrich, sear on both sides and set aside. Add the prawns and ostrich stock to the oil and sauté until cooked. Add the ostrich and sauce. Serve hot.

THE AMERICAN OSTRICH ASSOCIATION

RECIPE OF THE MONTH FOR SEPTEMBER 1998

Rolled Ostrich Steak with Sherry Baste

Serves 8

Stuffing
80 g (2¾ oz) cooked rice
4 spring onions, chopped
½ green pepper, seeded and chopped
15 ml (1 tbsp) tomato sauce
salt and freshly ground black pepper to taste
45 ml (3 tbsp) ostrich stock
(see recipe on page 11)

Basting mixture
45 ml (3 tbsp) each orange juice and sherry
25 ml (5 tsp) honey
10 ml (2 tsp) mustard powder

1.5 kg (3¼ lb) flat ostrich fillet
salt and freshly ground black pepper to taste

To prepare the stuffing, mix all the ingredients and set aside.

To prepare the baste, combine all the ingredients and set aside.

Place the fillet on a board and cover with stuffing. Roll up and tie with string. Rub salt and pepper into one side of the meat. Place the roll on the rack of an oven roasting pan and roast at 160 °C (325 °F, Gas Mark 3) for 15–20 minutes per 500 g (1 lb 2 oz) meat, plus 15 minutes for rare, or 20–25 minutes per 500 g (1 lb 2 oz), plus 20 minutes for medium done. Baste the meat regularly during the last 30 minutes.

Allow meat to rest in a warming drawer for 10 minutes. Remove the string and carve meat into thin slices. Serve with curried pumpkin and green peas.

SOURCE UNKNOWN

Ostrich Dijon

Serves 2

2 x 150 g (5½ oz) ostrich fillet steaks
1 ml (¼ tsp) pepper
20 ml (4 tsp) Dijon mustard
15 ml (1 tbsp) melted butter
1 ml (¼ tsp) garlic powder
5 ml (1 tsp) dried parsley
1 ml (¼ tsp) each dried rosemary,
paprika and dried thyme

Spray a large skillet with non-stick cooking spray. Place the skillet over medium heat and brown the steaks on both sides. Combine the remaining ingredients and spread over the meat. Cover and simmer. Continue basting with the sauce until the meat is medium-rare.

SOURCE UNKNOWN

Pot-roasted Ostrich Marinated with Mint and Soya

Serves 6

Marinade
700 ml (1¼ pints) good soy sauce (MSG free)
45 ml (3 tbsp) mint sauce
20 ml (4 tsp) green peppercorns, bruised
20 ml (4 tsp) chopped fresh ginger
30 ml (2 tbsp) apple-cider vinegar
salt and freshly ground black pepper

1 whole ostrich fillet

To prepare the marinade, combine all the ingredients in a large bowl. Place the fillet in the marinade, making sure it is submerged, and stand for approximately 8 hours.

Remove the fillet from the marinade and pat dry. In a heated, heavy-based pan, sear over high heat until a crust develops. Add 250 ml (9 fl oz) marinade, cover, reduce heat to low and cook for 15 minutes, turning twice.

Cut the fillet into thin slices and serve with stir-fried vegetables and rice noodles.

KLEIN KAROO LANDBOU CO-OPERATIVE, CHEF QUENTIN SPICKERNELL

Mustard and Chutney Meat Rolls

Serves 4

1 kg (2¼ lb) ostrich fillet, cooked
250 ml (9 fl oz) white vinegar
salt and freshly ground black pepper
apricot chutney
mustard
12 slices ham, sliced in half

Optional ingredients: pineapple chunks, 250 g (9 oz)
streaky bacon

Cool the meat and, when it is solid, cut into thin slices. Soak the slices in vinegar for 30 minutes and sprinkle with salt and pepper.

Remove fillet slices and smear chutney on one half and mustard on the other half. Place half a slice of ham on each slice and roll it up, pinning with a toothpick. Roast under the grill until heated through (about 8–10 minutes).

SOURCE UNKNOWN

VARIATION: Make kebabs, alternating with pineapple and bacon.

Sliced and Baked Ostrich Fillet

Serves 4

500 g (1 lb 2 oz) ostrich fillet, sliced and soaked
overnight in marinade
breadcrumbs
oil

Marinade
375 ml (13 fl oz) vinegar
375 ml (13 fl oz) oil
25 ml (5 tsp) Worcestershire sauce
20 ml (4 tsp) salt
10 ml (2 tsp) garlic salt
7 ml (1½ tsp) paprika
25 ml (5 tsp) tomato sauce
2 ml (½ tsp) mustard powder

Remove meat from the marinade. Place in cooking bag and bake in the oven at 230 °C (450 °F, Gas Mark 6) for 20–30 minutes until tender.

Remove the meat, roll the slices in breadcrumbs and fry in oil in a heavy-based pan for about 1 minute on each side until brown. Serve immediately.

SOURCE UNKNOWN

Sautéed Ostrich Steak with Spring Onions

Serves 4

175 g (6 oz) ostrich steak
10 ml (2 tsp) light soy sauce
10 ml (2 tsp) sugar
10 ml (2 tsp) dry sherry
10 ml (2 tsp) cornflour
2 ml (½ tsp) bicarbonate of soda
a pinch of freshly ground black pepper
75 ml (5 tbsp) water
60 ml (4 tbsp) oil, plus extra oil for deep frying
1 small onion, finely sliced
2 cloves garlic, sliced
2 medium-thick slices fresh root ginger, chopped
1 bunch spring onions, shredded
45 ml (3 tbsp) beef or ostrich stock
(see recipe on page 11)
15 ml (1 tbsp) oyster sauce
2 ml (½ tsp) dark soy sauce
5 ml (1 tsp) sesame oil (or sunflower oil)

Cut the steak into small, thin slices and marinate these for 2 hours in a mixture of light soy sauce, 5 ml (1 tsp) each sugar, sherry and cornflour, the bicarbonate of soda, pepper, 45 ml (3 tbsp) water and 30 ml (2 tbsp) oil.

Heat the oil for deep-frying, then add the meat and fry for a few minutes. Remove meat from pan and place on paper towel to drain excess oil. Set aside.

Heat 30 ml (2 tbsp) oil in a wok or frying pan, add the onion, garlic and ginger and fry until fragrant. Stir in the spring onions and meat and stir-fry for a few minutes.

Pour in the stock, remaining sherry and sugar, the oyster sauce, dark soy sauce, sesame oil and pepper to taste. Bring to the boil.

Blend the remaining cornflour with 30 ml (2 tbsp) water and stir this into the sauce. Simmer for 2 minutes. Transfer to a heated serving dish and serve immediately.

SOURCE UNKNOWN

Seared Ostrich set on Toasted Sunflower Polenta with Flash-fried Vegetables and Tapenade Sauce (pages 40–41)

Roast Ostrich with Chilli Sauce (page 53)

Roasts

Baked Ostrich

Serves 10–12

2–3 kg (4½–6½ lb) ostrich roast
60 ml (4 tbsp) vinegar
30 ml (2 tbsp) brown sugar
salt to taste
60 ml (4 tbsp) flour
125 g (4½ oz) butter, melted
250 ml (9 fl oz) water
125 ml (4½ fl oz) tomato sauce
30 ml (2 tbsp) Worcestershire sauce
1 clove garlic, crushed
75 ml (5 tbsp) very finely grated onion

Marinate the ostrich in a mixture of vinegar and sugar for 1 hour, turning frequently. Remove the meat and rub with salt. Toss in flour and then brown in a frying pan. Combine the remaining ingredients and pour over the meat. Bake at 180 °C (350 °F, Gas Mark 4) for 1 hour per kilogram (per 2¼ lb), basting frequently.

ORIENT BUTCHERY
MAGALIESBURG

Ostrich Roast with Pineapple

Serves 6–12

60 ml (4 tbsp) butter
165 ml (⅔ cup) flour
750 ml (1¼ pints) pineapple juice
250 ml (1 cup) apple jelly
1.5–3 kg (3¼–6½ lb) roast
1 x 410 g (14 oz) tin pineapple pieces, drained
500 ml (2 cups) diced green peppers
250 ml (1 cup) diced celery

Melt the butter in a large saucepan, add the flour and blend. Add the pineapple juice and apple jelly and bring to the boil. Remove from heat and cool. Pour the marinade into a large cooking dish, add the ostrich and marinate, covered, in the refrigerator overnight. Add the pineapple pieces, green peppers and celery and bake in a covered dish at 180 °C (350 °F, Gas mark 4) for 3 hours.

Serve with sweet-and-sour sauce as a topping and rice as a side dish.

SOURCE UNKNOWN

Sweet-and-Sour Ostrich

Serves 10

500 ml (18 fl oz) vinegar
500 ml (18 fl oz) red wine
125 ml (4½ fl oz) oil
1.5 litres (2¾ pints) water
1 large lemon, thinly sliced
2 ml (½ tsp) allspice
2 ml (½ tsp) whole peppercorns
1 clove garlic, crushed
2 medium onions, sliced
50 g (1¾ oz) brown sugar
3 kg (6½ lb) ostrich roast
250 ml (9 fl oz) sour cream
500 g (1 lb 2 oz) bacon fat

In a large bowl, combine all the ingredients, except the meat, cream and fat, and mix well. Place the meat in the sauce and marinate for 12 hours.

Remove the meat and reserve marinade. Melt the bacon fat in a large, heavy-based pan and brown the meat on all sides. Add 250 ml (9 fl oz) of the reserved marinade. Cook until tender – 1 hour per kilogram (per 2¼ lb) at 180 °C (350 °F, Gas Mark 4) – adding additional marinade as needed for basting. When the meat is tender, remove it from the pan. Add about 125 ml (½ cup) flour and the remaining marinade to the pan juices to make a thick gravy.

Stir in the sour cream shortly before serving.

ORIENT BUTCHERY
MAGALIESBURG

Apricot and Honey Ostrich Roast

Serves 8–10

2 kg (4½ lb) ostrich fillet or steak
500 g (1 lb 2 oz) pork belly, finely chopped
8 peppercorns
6 cloves
5 ml (1 tsp) dried thyme
125 ml (4½ fl oz) oil
125 ml (4½ fl oz) vinegar (or red wine)
15 ml (1 tbsp) salt
freshly ground black pepper to taste
60 ml (4 tbsp) flour
60 ml (4 tbsp) honey
1 x 765 g (1¾ lb) tin apricots, drained

Make incisions in the ostrich and stuff with pork belly, peppercorns and cloves. Sprinkle thyme over the meat, place in a covered dish and marinate for 24 hours in oil and vinegar. Turn the meat regularly and rub with salt and pepper.

Remove meat, wrap tightly in foil and place in a baking dish. Bake for 2 hours at 180 °C (350 °F, Gas Mark 4). Unwrap the foil and pour what is left of the oil and vinegar marinade over the top of the meat and bake for another 30 minutes. Slice the surface and smear with honey. Place apricots around the meat and bake for 30 minutes.

Serve with roast potatoes, vegetables and a salad.

Mrs C Nortier
Oudtshoorn

Whole Ostrich Buttock

Serves 50

For each 1.5 kg (3¼ lb) of roast:
375 g (13 oz) bacon and ham or pork fat, cubed
15 ml (1 tbsp) salt
2 ml (½ tsp) pepper
30 ml (2 tbsp) oil
15 ml (1 tbsp) sugar
250 ml (9 fl oz) meat extract or ostrich stock
(see recipe on page 11)
125 ml (4½ fl oz) tomato sauce
125 ml (4½ fl oz) vinegar, lemon juice or red wine
15 ml (1 tbsp) Worcestershire sauce
1 onion, finely chopped

Make as many incisions as possible in the ostrich roast and stuff with bacon or pork fat. Combine the remaining ingredients and marinate the meat for 2–3 days. Turn at least three times a day.

Cook the meat in the marinade at 180 °C (350 °F, Gas Mark 4) for 5–6 hours or until done. Baste regularly with sauce, adding water if necessary. Remove the meat from the dish when the gravy has cooled. Slice and serve warm, with the gravy served separately.

Klein Karoo Landbou Co-operative

Roast Fillet with Spices

Serves 6–8

45 ml (3 tbsp) coarse-grained prepared mustard
2 cloves garlic, minced*
7 ml (1 ½ tsp) dried oregano
2 ml (½ tsp) freshly ground black pepper
1 ostrich fillet

Preheat the oven to 200 °C (400 °F, Gas Mark 6).

Combine the mustard, garlic, oregano and pepper and rub this mixture over the surface of the fillet. At this stage, the roast may be covered and refrigerated for up to 24 hours before roasting to allow the different flavours to permeate the meat.

Place the roast in a shallow, foil-lined roasting pan and insert a meat thermometer in the thickest part of the roast. Roast for 15 minutes, then reduce the temperature to 160 °C (325 °F, Gas Mark 3) and roast for about 40 minutes or until the thermometer registers 70 °C (160 °F) for medium done.

Place the roast on a cutting board, cover with foil and leave to stand for 10 minutes before carving.

Carve into very thin slices and serve immediately.

SOURCE UNKNOWN

* FOR A STRONGER FLAVOUR INSIDE THE MEAT, CUT THE GARLIC INTO SLIVERS AND INSERT THEM INTO SMALL POCKETS CUT AT RANDOM INTERVALS ALL OVER THE ROAST.

Roast Ostrich Fillet in Aspic

Serves 6

1 kg (2 ¼ lb) ostrich fillet
45–60 ml (3–4 tbsp) oil for roasting
100 g (3 ½ oz) button mushrooms
30 ml (2 tbsp) olive oil
275 ml (10 fl oz) aspic jelly*

Coat the roasting pan with oil and roast the fillet at 220 °C (425 °F, Gas Mark 6) for about 40 minutes. Allow to cool.

Wash the mushrooms and then sauté in olive oil for 1 minute only. Tip them onto a plate and allow to cool. Drain on a paper towel.

Carve the fillet, arrange in overlapping slices around a flat serving dish and garnish with the mushrooms. Brush well with cold, but still liquid, aspic, covering the fillet completely. Leave to set and serve cold.

SOURCE UNKNOWN

* THIS CAN BE MADE FROM COMMERCIAL ASPIC POWDER, ADDING A GLASS OF SHERRY IN PLACE OF THE WATER.

Roast Ostrich with Chilli Sauce

Serves 10–12

2 kg (4½ lb) ostrich roast
4 cloves garlic, minced
2 ml (½ tsp) freshly ground black pepper
2 large onions, peeled and cut into 6 mm (¼ in) slices
1 bottle of your favourite chilli sauce
180 ml (6¼ fl oz) ostrich stock
(see recipe on page 11), beer or water
30 ml (2 tbsp) Worcestershire sauce
15 ml (1 tbsp) packed brown sugar

Preheat the oven to 180 °C (350 °F, Gas Mark 4). Place the meat in a shallow roasting pan. Spread the garlic evenly over the meat and then sprinkle with pepper.

Separate the onion slices into rings and arrange over the meat. Combine the remaining ingredients and pour over the meat and onions.

Cover the roast with heavy-duty foil or a roasting pan lid. Roast for 2 hours. Turn over the meat and stir the onions into the sauce. Spoon the sauce over the meat. Cover and roast for 1–2 hours more or until fork tender.

Transfer the roast to a cutting board, cover with foil and allow to stand for 10 minutes.

Carve the meat thinly and serve with the juices from the roasting pan.

SOURCE UNKNOWN

Casseroles

Ostrich Stew

Serves 4–6

vegetable oil or olive oil
2 onions, finely chopped
4 cloves garlic, finely chopped
2 kg (4½ lb) ostrich goulash
100 g (3½ oz) bacon, chopped
4 carrots, thinly sliced
575 ml (1 pint) red wine
15 ml (1 tbsp) tomato purée
a good splash Schnapps
2 bay leaves
1 large piece boerewors (sausage)
100 g (3½ oz) mushrooms, quartered

Heat some oil in a large pan. Add the onions and garlic and cook gently for a few minutes until the onions are soft and translucent. Add the goulash and brown. Add the remaining ingredients, except the boerewors and mushrooms, and simmer for 10–15 minutes. Add the boerewors and mushrooms and simmer for 20 minutes. Serve with brown rice and a salad.

SOURCE UNKNOWN

Ostrich Sausage Casserole

Serves 8

1 kg (2¼ lb) ostrich mince
120 g (4 oz) pork sausages
2 cloves garlic, chopped
2 onions, chopped
freshly ground black pepper to taste
30 ml (2 tbsp) dried sweet basil
1 green pepper, chopped
1 x 410 g (14 oz) tin sliced mushrooms, drained
120 g (4 oz) uncooked macaroni
60 ml (4 tbsp) olive oil
125 g (4½ oz) ripe black olives, sliced
2 x 410 g (14 oz) tins chopped tomatoes
1 x 410 g (14 oz) tin sweetcorn, drained
250 g (9 oz) grated Parmesan cheese

Brown the ostrich and sausages together in a large pan. Crumble the meat and drain excess fat. Add remaining ingredients, except the cheese, and mix well.

Place in a baking dish, sprinkle with cheese and bake, covered with foil, at 180 °C (350 °F, Gas Mark 4) for 45 minutes. Uncover and cook for a further 15 minutes until a crust forms on top.

SOURCE UNKNOWN

Ostrich and Macaroni Casserole

Serves 8

400 g (14 oz) onions, sliced
20 ml (4 tsp) oil
1 kg (2¼ lb) ostrich steaks, thinly sliced
15 g (½ oz) flour
1 x 410 g (14 oz) tin tomatoes, diced
550 g (1¼ lb) cooked macaroni
5 ml (1 tsp) paprika
2 ml (½ tsp) nutmeg
1 clove garlic, crushed (or 1 ml/¼ tsp garlic powder)
5 ml (1 tsp) salt
2 ml (½ tsp) freshly ground black pepper
250 ml (9 fl oz) low-fat plain yoghurt

Sauté the onions in oil until soft and translucent. Add the ostrich steaks and flour. Stir and sauté for about 2 minutes. Pour the mixture into a casserole dish. Add the tomatoes, macaroni, paprika, nutmeg, garlic and seasoning.

Cover and bake at 160 °C (325 °F, Gas Mark 3) for about 1 hour or until tender. Remove from oven and stir in the yoghurt. Serve piping hot.

WEIGH-LESS MAGAZINE, DECEMBER 1997

Ostrich Curry

Serves 8

oil for frying
2 kg (4½ lb) ostrich goulash
20 ml (4 tsp) curry powder
10 ml (2 tsp) each turmeric,
ground coriander and ground ginger
10 ml (2 tsp) sugar
10 ml (2 tsp) salt
5 ml (1 tsp) pepper
45 ml (3 tbsp) sultanas
250 ml (1 cup) finely chopped apple
45 ml (3 tbsp) fruit chutney
4 lemon leaves, bruised
2 cloves garlic, finely chopped
1 onion, finely chopped
250 ml (1 cup) skinned, squeezed and
coarsely chopped ripe tomatoes
8 potatoes, diced
water

Heat the oil in a large saucepan and brown the meat.

In a mixing bowl, combine the curry powder, turmeric, coriander, ginger, sugar, salt, pepper, sultanas, apple and chutney. Add to the saucepan, mixing well, then add the lemon leaves, garlic, onion and tomatoes.

Simmer, covered, until the meat is almost tender (about 1½ hours), adding a little water if it becomes too dry. Add the potatoes and cook for 30 minutes, adding more water if necessary. Check seasoning and serve with boiled rice and sambals, such as ground coconut, diced tomato and onion, bananas in cream and chutney.

SOURCE UNKNOWN

Curried Ostrich Neck

Serves 6

15 ml (1 tbsp) chopped fat
1 carrot, finely grated
1 onion, grated
1 kg (2¼ lb) cooked ostrich neck, thinly sliced
15 ml (1 tbsp) salt
125 ml (½ cup) dried apricots, soaked overnight
15 ml (1 tbsp) curry powder
5 ml (1 tsp) turmeric
2 ml (½ tsp) ginger
a pinch of cayenne pepper
60 ml (4 tbsp) vinegar
30 ml (2 tbsp) sugar
15 ml (1 tbsp) cornflour
4 lemon leaves, bruised

In a large saucepan, melt the fat and fry the carrot and onion until brown. Add the ostrich and brown. Add salt and enough water to cover the meat, then stew slowly over low heat, covered, for 30 minutes.

In a separate saucepan, mix the remaining ingredients and cook for 8–10 minutes. Add the mixture to the meat and stew for 10 minutes. Remove and discard lemon leaves before serving.

Potato cubes, cooked separately, can be added in with the carrot and onion, if desired.

Klein Karoo Landbou Co-operative

Tomato Stewed Ostrich Neck

Serves 4

30 ml (2 tbsp) chopped pork fat
1 carrot, grated
1 onion, grated
1 kg (2¼ lb) cooked ostrich neck, thinly sliced
5 ml (1 tsp) salt
170 g (6 oz) peeled, diced tomatoes or
½ x 110 g (4 oz) tin tomato purée
2 ml (½ tsp) fine cloves (or to taste)
5 ml (1 tsp) whole peppercorns
250 ml (9 fl oz) milk
30 ml (2 tbsp) sugar
5 ml (1 tsp) cornflour

Melt the fat, add the carrot and onion and fry until brown. Add the ostrich and brown. Add salt and enough water to cover the meat, and stew for 1¼ hours.

In another saucepan, cook the remaining ingredients, except the milk, sugar and cornflour. When the meat is tender, add the tomato mixture and cook for 10 minutes. The milk, sugar and cornflour should be added just before serving.

Potatoes can be cooked and added in with the tomato if desired.

Klein Karoo Landbou Co-operative

Ostrich Neck with Dumplings

Serves 6

1 ostrich neck, sliced
5 ml (1 tsp) salt (or to taste)
1 ml (¼ tsp) freshly ground black pepper (or to taste)
8–10 cloves
1 sprig of mint
a few celery leaves
enough water to cover meat

Dumplings
250 ml (1 cup) flour
125 ml (½ cup) self-raising flour
a pinch of salt
25 ml (5 tsp) butter
250 ml (9 fl oz) boiling water

To make the stew, combine all the ingredients and cook over low heat for 3–4 hours or until tender. Remove celery leaves before serving.

To make the dumplings, mix all the ingredients with boiling water until the mixture forms a smooth dough. Place large spoonfuls into the stew and cook until done.

Serve with rice.

MRS A VON BLERK
MALMESBURY

Ostrich Neck with Dried Fruit

Serves 8

250 ml (9 fl oz) meat extract
250 ml (9 fl oz) muscadel
500 g (1 lb 2 oz) mixed dried fruit
30 ml (2 tbsp) olive oil
2 large leeks, sliced
2.5 kg (5½ lb) ostrich neck, cut into pieces
5 ml (1 tsp) dried coriander
4 cloves
4 cardamom seeds, bruised
1 bay leaf
100 ml (3½ fl oz) balsamic vinegar
1 kg (2¼ lb) waterblommetjies,
soaked in salt water for about 1 hour
(if unavailable, substitute broccoli or baby cabbage)
4 medium onions, quartered
5 medium sweet potatoes, diced

Mix the meat extract and muscadel and soak the dried fruit in this mixture for 30 minutes or until swollen.

Heat the oil in saucepan and fry the leeks until they begin to soften slightly. Add the ostrich and seal. Add the herbs and vinegar and simmer for 5 minutes, then add the fruit mix and simmer until half cooked. Add the waterblommetjies, onions and sweet potatoes, cover and stew over medium heat until cooked.

MARIETJIE THERON OF WORCESTER
WON THE SAFARI DRIED FRUIT COMPETITION WITH THIS RECIPE.

Ostrich Neck and Bean Casserole with Thyme

Serves 6

3 medium onions
1 leek
3 stalks celery
3 turnips
1 x 410 g (14 oz) tin whole tomatoes
15 ml (1 tbsp) olive oil
300 ml (11 fl oz) red wine
300 ml (11 fl oz) ostrich stock
(see recipe on page 11), or beef stock
1.2 kg (2¾ lb) ostrich neck, sliced
250 ml (1 cup) dried haricot beans, soaked overnight
30 ml (2 tbsp) thyme sprigs
10 ml (2 tsp) chilli sauce
8 cloves garlic
salt and freshly ground black pepper to taste

Shred the onions, leek, celery, turnips and tomatoes in a food processor, then sauté in olive oil until softened. Add the wine and stock and simmer for 5 minutes. Add the neck, cover and simmer for approximately 2½ hours.

Rinse the beans in cold water and stir them into the casserole. Replace the lid and simmer for 1½ hours. Add the thyme, chilli sauce, garlic and seasoning. Simmer for 10 minutes, making sure the meat is sufficiently tender and the beans soft.

KLEIN KAROO LANDBOU CO-OPERATIVE, CHEF QUENTIN SPICKERNELL

Braised Ostrich Neck

Serves 6

1.5 kg (3¼ lb) ostrich neck
salt and freshly ground black pepper
flour
45 ml (3 tbsp) oil
500 ml (18 fl oz) water
15 ml (1 tbsp) vinegar
4 potatoes, cut into quarters, lengthways
3 carrots, cut into wedges

Toss the meat in salt, pepper and flour, and sauté in hot oil until browned. Add the water and vinegar, cover and cook slowly for 3–4 hours. The potatoes and carrots can be added 30 minutes before the end of the cooking time.

ORIENT BUTCHERY
MAGALIESBURG

Braised Ostrich with Pecan Nuts and Celery

Serves 8

1.2 kg (2¾ lb) ostrich steak
45 ml (3 tbsp) olive oil
4 large stalks celery, cut into 2 cm (¾ in) pieces
150 g (5½ oz) pecan nuts
200 ml (7 fl oz) red wine
250 ml (9 fl oz) chicken stock
3 large onions, chopped
2 bay leaves
60 ml (4 tbsp) blackcurrant jelly or cranberry jelly
25 ml (5 tsp) lemon peel or zest
salt and freshly ground black pepper to taste

Cut the steak into paper-thin slices of about 100 g (3½ oz) each. Seal the meat quickly in half the oil.

Remove the meat and set aside. Add the rest of the oil and pan-fry the celery. Add the nuts, stirring continuously over high heat until a nutty flavour develops. Pour in the wine and cook until the liquid is reduced by half, then add the stock and cook until it is reduced by two-thirds.

Add the meat and remaining ingredients and reheat, stirring well.

Serve with mashed potato, pumpkin or sweet potatoes.

SOURCE UNKNOWN

Ostrich Fillet Casserole

Serves 4

1 kg (2¼ lb) ostrich steak, cubed
125 ml (4½ fl oz) vinegar
6 onions, sliced
45 ml (3 tbsp) oil
salt and freshly ground black pepper
15 ml (1 tbsp) Worcestershire sauce
30 ml (2 tbsp) tomato purée
15 ml (1 tbsp) flour
1 bouillon cube

Tenderise the meat, sprinkle it with vinegar and leave to marinate for at least 30 minutes. Place a layer of onions in the bottom of a casserole dish with the oil. Place slices of meat on top and add another layer of onions. Mix the Worcestershire sauce, tomato purée and flour in a cup and fill with the prepared bouillon cube. Pour over the meat and bake at 140 °C (275 °F, Gas Mark ½) for 2–3 hours or until tender. You can add potatoes or squash in the last 30 minutes if desired.

KLEIN KAROO LANDBOU CO-OPERATIVE

Ostrich Stroganoff with Topping

Serves 4

1 onion, chopped
1 clove garlic, crushed
4–5 rashers bacon, chopped
20 ml (4 tsp) butter
250 g (9 oz) mushrooms, sliced
500 g (1 lb 2 oz) ostrich fillet, cut in thin strips
90 ml (6 tbsp) seasoned flour
250 ml (9 fl oz) ostrich stock (see recipe on page 11)
salt and freshly ground black pepper
1 ml (¼ tsp) paprika
125 ml (4½ fl oz) sour cream
20 ml (4 tsp) chopped parsley to garnish

Topping
1 large egg
125 ml (4½ fl oz) milk
125 ml (4½ fl oz) sunflower oil
250 ml (1 cup) flour, sifted
10 ml (2 tsp) baking powder
5 ml (1 tsp) salt

Sauté the onion, garlic and bacon in heated butter. Add the mushrooms and stir-fry for a few minutes. Remove from pan and set aside.

Toss stroganoff strips in seasoned flour and brown in the pan. Add the onion mixture and ostrich stock. Simmer until meat is tender (about 45–60 minutes). Season with salt, pepper and paprika. Stir in the sour cream and reheat slowly.

While the meat is simmering, prepare the topping. Beat the egg, milk and oil, then sift the dry ingredients into this mixture and beat well until the batter is smooth.

When the meat is ready, place in a casserole dish. Spoon over the topping and bake at 180 °C (350 °F, Gas Mark 4) for 30 minutes or until topping is well risen, firm and brown. Garnish and serve immediately.

RON HENDERSON
MAGALIES OSTRICH RANCH, KROONDAL

Tasty Mushroom and Ostrich Goulash

Serves 4

750 g (1¾ lb) ostrich steak, cubed
10 ml (2 tsp) salt
1 ml (¼ tsp) black pepper
60 ml (4 tbsp) flour
30 ml (2 tbsp) oil
2 onions, sliced
425 ml (¾ pint) mushroom soup
125 ml (4½ fl oz) meat extract
(or ostrich stock, see recipe on page 11)
280 g (10 oz) mushrooms, chopped
30 ml (2 tbsp) vinegar
125 ml (½ cup) grated Cheddar cheese

Roll the cubed meat in a mixture of salt, pepper and flour. Fry until brown in hot oil with the onions. Add the soup and simmer for 30 minutes. Add the meat extract and simmer slowly for 15 minutes, then add the mushrooms and vinegar and cook until tender – about 2 hours. Spoon into a bowl, sprinkle with cheese and serve immediately.

KLEIN KAROO LANDBOU CO-OPERATIVE

Ostrich Bourguignon

Serves 8

1.5 kg (3¼ lb) ostrich steak,
cut into 25 mm (1 in) cubes
250 g (9 oz) pork (with some fat),
cut into 6 mm (¼ in) thick strips
60 ml (4 tbsp) vegetable oil
3 carrots, sliced
60 ml (4 tbsp) flour
750 ml (1¼ pints) red wine
10 ml (2 tsp) salt
10 ml (2 tsp) freshly ground black pepper
2 cloves garlic, peeled and cut in half
15 ml (1 tbsp) tomato paste
1 bay leaf
5 ml (1 tsp) fresh or ground thyme
6 medium-sized fresh mushrooms, sliced
250 g (9 oz) small onions, peeled

In a large, heavy skillet, sauté the ostrich and pork in oil. Place the carrots in the skillet and brown them briefly. Stir in the flour. Pour in the wine and simmer for 1 minute, scraping the side and bottom well. Add the remaining ingredients, cover and simmer for 2 hours. Remove the bay leaf before serving.

AMERICAN OSTRICH ASSOCIATION

Ostrich, Onion and Orange Casserole

Serves 4

1 kg (2¼ lb) ostrich steak, cubed
12–15 baby onions
45 ml (3 tbsp) port
250 ml (9 fl oz) beef stock
250 ml (9 fl oz) orange juice
6 cloves garlic
25 ml (5 tsp) orange zest
3 cloves
3 pimento berries
2 bay leaves
1 stick cinnamon
30 ml (2 tbsp) butter
cornflour
salt and freshly ground black pepper

In a heavy-based saucepan, lightly sear the steak cubes, then remove from the pan and set aside. Braise the onions until browned and remove from pan.

Add the port and simmer until reduced by half. Add the stock and orange juice and simmer until reduced by two-thirds. Add the remaining ingredients, except the cornflour and seasoning and simmer for approximately 10 minutes over medium heat.

Add the steak and onions and leave uncovered, stirring occasionally. Mix the cornflour with a little cold water and thicken the sauce accordingly. Season.

Serve with either fragrant Thai rice, basmati rice or mashed potatoes.

KLEIN KAROO LANDBOU CO-OPERATIVE, CHEF QUENTIN SPICKERNELL

Ostrich Stroganoff

Serves 6

1 kg (2¼ lb) ostrich steak
60 ml (4 tbsp) butter
250 g (9 oz) mushrooms, sliced
125 ml (4½ fl oz) tomato juice
1 clove garlic, crushed
salt to taste
5 ml (1 tsp) pepper
300 ml (11 fl oz) mushroom soup
250 ml (9 fl oz) sour cream

Cut the ostrich into 2 cm (¾ in) strips and brown in butter. Add the mushrooms and tomato juice. Cover and simmer for 30 minutes. Add the remaining ingredients and simmer for 1 hour. Serve with rice or buttered noodles.

ORIENT BUTCHERY
MAGALIESBURG

Ostrich Breyani

Serves 6

25 ml (5 tsp) ginger/garlic masala
30 ml (2 tbsp) Breyani mix
125 ml (4½ fl oz) yoghurt
30 ml (2 tbsp) lemon juice or vinegar
2 ml (½ tsp) turmeric
5 ml (1 tsp) salt (or to taste)
4 green chillies, cut into pieces (optional)
1.5 kg (3¼ lb) ostrich fillet, cubed
500 ml (2 cups) brown lentils
750 ml (3 cups) rice (white or basmati)
15 ml (1 tbsp) mixed spices
8 small potatoes, halved or quartered
2 medium onions, sliced
180 ml (6¼ fl oz) oil
4 hard-boiled eggs, sliced

In a large dish, mix the masala, Breyani mix, yoghurt, lemon juice, turmeric, salt and green chillies. Add the ostrich and mix well. Leave the meat to marinate in the spices for a few hours.

In the meantime, cook the lentils in boiling salted water, then drain. Boil the rice with the mixed spices, but leave slightly underdone.

Fry the potatoes and onions in the oil until they are a light yellow in colour.

In a pot with a splash of oil, spread a handful of rice and lentils over the bottom. Cover this with meat, then spread the balance of the lentils over the meat, then the potatoes and a third of the remaining rice. Arrange a layer of sliced eggs on top and cover with another third of the remaining rice. You can also sprinkle a few onion flakes over the rice, if desired.

Sprinkle with 30 ml (2 tbsp) oil and 125 ml (4½ fl oz) water, cover and place the pot on high heat for about 10 minutes, then reduce heat and simmer for 1 hour.

Serve hot with the remaining rice.

ZARINA SALOGEE
RUSTENBURG

Koeloe (Ostrich and Tomato Stew)

Serves 4

750 g (1¾ lb) ostrich steak, cubed or goulash
5 ml (1 tsp) salt
freshly ground black pepper to taste
30 ml (2 tbsp) flour
3 onions, chopped
4 cloves
60 ml (4 tbsp) oil
250 ml (9 fl oz) boiling water
6 potatoes, diced
8 tomatoes, peeled and chopped

Cover the meat with seasoned flour. Fry the onions and cloves in the oil, add the meat and fry until brown. Add the boiling water and simmer for 1 hour. Add the potatoes and tomatoes and simmer for about 1 hour until all the ingredients are tender.

KLEIN KAROO LANDBOU CO-OPERATIVE

VARIATION: Add 1 x 285 g (10¼ oz) tin mushroom soup or creamed mushrooms.

Ostrich Bredie

Serves 6

45 ml (3 tbsp) oil
1 kg (2¼ lb) ostrich steak,
cut into 2.5 cm (1 in) cubes
500 g (1 lb 2 oz) lamb, cut into 2.5 cm (1 in) cubes
1 onion, finely chopped
2 stalks celery, finely chopped
salt and freshly ground black pepper
spices of your choice

Sauce

1 packet cream of tomato soup
4 tomatoes, peeled and diced
2 potatoes, peeled and diced
250 g (9 oz) fresh mushrooms, halved
200 ml (7 fl oz) ginger ale
25 ml (5 tsp) Worcestershire sauce

Warm the oil in a heavy skillet and fry the meat and onion. Add the celery and sauté. Add the seasoning and spices and cook until tender.

To prepare the sauce, mix the soup according to the packet instructions. Add the remaining ingredients and combine with the meat mixture. Cook until done.

Serve with maize rice or plain rice and salad.

JOEY GOOSEN
RUSTENBURG

Ostrich Medallions with Kahlúa Cream Sauce (page 34)

Ostrich Sasheem (page 114)

Oriental Ostrich Meatballs in Sweet-and-Sour Sauce (page 18)

Braised Ostrich with Pecan Nuts and Celery (page 59)

Mince

Ostrich Shepherd Pie

Serves 4

60 ml (4 tbsp) olive oil
500 g (1 lb 2 oz) ostrich mince
125 g (4½ oz) shoulder bacon, diced
1 large onion, chopped
1 large green pepper, diced
140 g (5 oz) frozen mixed vegetables
1 x 410 g (14 oz) tin whole tomatoes, drained
and chopped
15 ml (1 tbsp) tomato sauce
15 ml (1 tbsp) Worcestershire sauce
1 packet oxtail soup mix
7 ml (1½ tsp) mixed dried herbs
freshly ground black pepper to taste

Topping
6 large potatoes, cooked and peeled
30 ml (2 tbsp) butter or margarine
100 ml (3½ fl oz) milk
salt and freshly ground black pepper to taste

Preheat oven to 180 °C (350 °F, Gas Mark 4). Heat 45 ml (3 tbsp) oil in a pan and brown the mince and bacon. Remove from stove and set aside.

Heat the remaining oil and fry the onion and green pepper until soft. Combine the remaining ingredients and add to the meat, mixing well. Spoon the mixture into an ovenproof dish and set aside.

To make the topping, mix the potatoes, butter, milk and seasoning, and beat until smooth. Spoon the potato topping evenly over the meat. (You can also sprinkle grated cheese and breadcrumbs on top if desired.) Bake for 30 minutes until golden brown.

Serve with green peas and a salad.

SARIE, 6 NOVEMBER 1996

Ostrich Mushroom Roll

Serves 6

Dough
500 ml (2 cups) flour
30 ml (2 tbsp) baking powder
1 ml (¼ tsp) salt
180 g (6½ oz) butter or margarine
1 egg
your favourite mustard

500 ml (2 cups) cooked ostrich mince
a pinch of nutmeg
1 ml (¼ tsp) dried thyme
1 beef stock cube
250 ml (9 fl oz) water
1 x 285 g (10¼ oz) tin mushroom soup

For the dough, sift the dry ingredients and rub in butter. Mix with egg. Roll out the dough and spread with mustard.
Mix the mince with nutmeg and thyme and spread it over the dough. Make into a roll. Place in an ovenproof dish and pour over the beef stock cube dissolved in the water. Pour mushroom soup over and bake at 190 °C (375 °F, Gas Mark 4) until nicely browned and cooked (about 45 minutes).

SOURCE UNKNOWN

Ostrich Meatloaf

Serves 6

1 egg, beaten
700 g (1½ lb) ostrich mince
100 g (3½ oz) low-fat cheese, grated
120 g (4 oz) oats, uncooked
60 ml (4 tbsp) water
1 ml (¼ tsp) dried oregano
180 g (6½ oz) canned tomato paste

Combine all ingredients, except the tomato paste, and mix lightly. Shape into a loaf in a 25 x 15 cm (9¾ x 6 in) baking dish. Bake at 180 °C (350 °F, Gas Mark 4) for 1 hour. Top with tomato paste and leave to stand for about 10 minutes before serving.

WEIGH-LESS MAGAZINE, DECEMBER 1997

Ostrich Steak Tartare

Serves 4

1 kg (2¼ lb) ostrich steak, minced
5 ml (1 tsp) freshly ground black pepper
7 ml (1½ tsp) salt
45–75 ml (3–5 tbsp) oil
15 ml (1 tbsp) wine vinegar
5 ml (1 tsp) prepared mustard
dash of Tabasco sauce
4 shallots, chopped
4 gherkins, chopped
30 ml (2 tbsp) chopped capers
4 egg yolks
2 gherkins, sliced
2 hard-boiled eggs, yolk removed and chopped
chopped parsley

Place the mince and seasoning in a large bowl and work together well with the oil, vinegar, mustard and Tabasco. Add half the shallots, chopped gherkins and 15 ml (1 tbsp) capers. When thoroughly mixed, spoon a quarter of the mixture onto each plate, make a depression in the centre and place an egg yolk in this. Garnish plates with the remaining shallots, sliced gherkins, leftover capers and chopped egg white. Each guest then mixes in the egg yolk with the other ingredients, adding seasoning, oil, vinegar and mustard according to taste. The parsley and crumbled egg yolk are sprinkled on before eating.

SOURCE UNKNOWN

Ostrich Bobotie

Serves 8

1 slice white bread
250 ml (9 fl oz) milk
1 kg (2¼ lb) ostrich mince
1 medium onion, finely chopped
125 ml (½ cup) seedless raisins
125 ml (½ cup) blanched almonds
15 ml (1 tbsp) apricot jam
15 ml (1 tbsp) fruit chutney
25 ml (5 tsp) lemon juice
10 ml (2 tsp) curry powder
5 ml (1 tsp) turmeric
10 ml (2 tsp) salt
10 ml (2 tsp) butter or oil
3 eggs
2 bay leaves

Soak the bread in 125 ml (4½ fl oz) milk, squeeze to remove the milk, then mix the bread with the mince. Mix in all remaining ingredients, except the butter, eggs, milk and bay leaves. Melt the butter or heat the oil in a frying pan and lightly brown the meat mixture. Turn out into a casserole dish.

Beat the eggs together with the rest of the milk and pour over the meat. Garnish with bay leaves. Bake at 180 °C (350 °F, Gas Mark 4) until set (about 50 minutes).

KLEIN KAROO LANDBOU CO-OPERATIVE

Ostrich Mince and Wine Pie

Serves 6

8 slices white bread
250 ml (9 fl oz) white wine
400 g (14 oz) Cheddar cheese, grated
750 ml (3 cups) spiced cooked ostrich mince
salt, pepper, nutmeg and garlic to taste
4 eggs
750 ml (1¼ pints) milk

Soak the bread in wine. Butter a dish and layer with bread and cheese. Top with a layer of meat and sprinkle with salt, pepper, garlic and nutmeg. Repeat again with bread, wine, cheese, meat and spices.

Beat the eggs and milk together and pour over the meat. Bake at 180 °C (350 °F, Gas Mark 4) for 40 minutes.

KLEIN KAROO LANDBOU CO-OPERATIVE

Teriyaki Ostrich Mince Balls

Serves 4

3 spring onions, chopped
5 ml (1 tsp) garlic powder
5 ml (1 tsp) grated ginger
60 ml (4 tbsp) soy sauce
15 ml (1 tbsp) sugar
500 g (1 lb 2 oz) ostrich mince
15 ml (1 tbsp) oil
90 ml (6 tbsp) water
15 ml (1 tbsp) cornflour

Combine the onions, garlic, ginger, soy sauce and sugar and mix half of it with the mince. Shape the mince mixture into 12 meatballs. Heat the oil and fry the meatballs over medium heat, turning often until brown. Remove from pan and keep warm.

Mix the water and cornflour and add to pan with the remaining soy mixture. Stir until the sauce thickens and bubbles. Boil for 1 minute.

Pour sauce over the meatballs and serve immediately. Ideal with rice, mange tout (snow peas) and carrots.

RON HENDERSON
MAGALIES OSTRICH RANCH, KROONDAL

Ostrich Meatballs with Mustard Sauce

Serves 6

Meatballs

1 kg (2¼ lb) ostrich mince
250 g (9 oz) rindless bacon, diced
30 ml (2 tbsp) scorched coriander
salt and freshly ground black pepper to taste
60 ml (4 tbsp) vinegar
grated lemon rind
75 ml (5 tbsp) coarsely grated onion
1 egg, beaten
125 ml (½ cup) fresh breadcrumbs
grated cheese
finely chopped parsley

Mustard sauce

15 ml (1 tbsp) butter
15 ml (1 tbsp) cornflour
salt and freshly ground black pepper to taste
250 ml (9 fl oz) milk
75 ml (5 tbsp) beef or ostrich stock
(see recipe on page 11)
5 ml (1 tsp) mustard powder
1 egg yolk
125 ml (½ cup) grated Cheddar cheese

To make the meatballs, mix all the ingredients well. Mould meatballs and bake at 180 °C (350 °F, Gas Mark 4) for approximately 45 minutes in a buttered ovenproof dish covered with foil. Remove foil 15 minutes before the end to brown the meatballs. (To prevent the oil from spluttering, add a drop or two of vinegar.) Arrange in a serving dish and keep warm.

To prepare the sauce, melt the butter, add cornflour, salt and pepper and stir until smooth. Boil for 1 minute. Add the milk and stock and stir until the sauce thickens. Mix the mustard and egg yolk and add it to the milk mixture. Stir over low heat until thick and smooth, then stir in the cheese until melted.

Pour sauce over the meatballs, sprinkle with grated cheese and brown under the grill. Garnish with parsley.

Klein Karoo Landbou Co-operative

Ostrich Mince Lasagne

Serves 6

Meat sauce

15 ml (1 tbsp) olive oil
1 medium onion, chopped
1 medium carrot, chopped
1 stalk celery, finely chopped
2 cloves garlic, crushed
750 g (1¾ lb) ostrich mince
75 ml (5 tbsp) red wine
35 g (1¼ oz) tomato paste
1 x 410 g (14 oz) tin tomato, garlic and basil mix
(or own choice)
125 ml (4½ fl oz) water
4 slices ham or bacon, diced
15 ml (1 tbsp) dried oregano
30 ml (2 tbsp) chopped parsley

Cheese sauce

125 ml (½ cup) cake flour
125 g (4½ oz) butter
1 litre (1¾ pints) lukewarm milk
60 g (2 oz) Parmesan cheese, grated
pinch of nutmeg

18 sheets lasagne
40 g (1½ oz) Cheddar cheese, grated

Heat the oil in a deep frying pan. Add the onion, carrot, celery and garlic and sauté until soft. Add the mince and sauté until golden brown. Add the wine and boil until the wine has evaporated. Stir in the tomato paste, tomato mix and water. Reduce heat and simmer uncovered until mixture is thick. Stir in bacon or ham and the herbs.

For the cheese sauce, melt the butter in a pot. Remove from heat and gradually stir in the flour to form a smooth paste. Return to low heat and cook for 2 minutes. Remove from heat and very gradually add the milk. Return to low heat until the mixture boils and thickens. Remove from heat and stir in the nutmeg and cheese until melted and smooth.

Grease a shallow, square ovenproof dish that should be large enough to take two sheets of lasagne side by side without overlap. Add enough cheese sauce to cover the base of the dish. Place 2 sheets of lasagne on top and then spread the mince mixture over the lasagne. Repeat layers, finishing with a layer of cheese sauce. Sprinkle with Cheddar cheese and stand for 2 hours.

Bake at 180 °C (350 °F, Gas Mark 4) until the pasta is soft and the cheese golden brown.

RON HENDERSON
MAGALIES OSTRICH RANCH, KROONDAL

Curry Meatballs with Banana Sauce

Serves 6

Meatballs
1 kg (2¼ lb) ostrich mince
salt and freshly ground black pepper
15 ml (1 tbsp) vinegar
grated nutmeg and cloves
4 slices white bread
500 ml (18 fl oz) water
2 eggs
flour
3 bananas

Banana sauce
3 medium onions, finely chopped
lard or butter
30 ml (2 tbsp) flour
180 ml (6¼ fl oz) vinegar
125 ml (4½ fl oz) water
20 ml (4 tsp) curry powder
15 ml (1 tbsp) turmeric
30 ml (2 tbsp) sugar
salt and freshly ground black pepper
45 ml (3 tbsp) apricot jam
3 bananas, finely sliced
1 green or red pepper, chopped

Mix the mince with salt, pepper, vinegar, nutmeg and cloves to taste. Soak the bread in water, crumble and add with the water to the mince. Beat eggs and add, lightly kneading the mixture. Roll meatballs and dip in flour. Arrange the meatballs spaciously in a baking dish and slice the bananas over the top.

To make the sauce, fry the onions in butter or lard until lightly browned. Stir in the flour and add the remaining ingredients. Cook the sauce until the bananas are soft.

Pour the sauce over the meatballs and bake at 150 °C (300 °F, Gas Mark 1) for 1 hour. Serve with rice and stewed dried peaches.

Klein Karoo Landbou Co-operative

Ostrich Mince Roll

Serves 6

Filling

1 onion, chopped
1 clove garlic, crushed
500 g (1 lb 2 oz) ostrich mince
125 g (4½ oz) mushrooms, sliced
1 potato, chopped in small cubes
1 carrot, finely sliced
2 stalks celery, finely sliced
salt and freshly ground black pepper to taste

Dough

500 ml (2 cups) cake flour
5 ml (1 tsp) baking powder
2 ml (½ tsp) salt
5 ml (1 tsp) cayenne pepper
90 ml (6 tbsp) butter
250 ml (1 cup) grated cheese
1 egg
75 ml (5 tbsp) milk

1 egg, beaten
parsley to garnish

For the filling, fry the onion and garlic until translucent. Add the remaining ingredients and simmer until cooked. If necessary, thicken with a little gravy powder or cornflour and cool completely.

For the dough, sift the dry ingredients. Rub the butter into the flour until it resembles fine breadcrumbs. Add the cheese. Beat the egg and milk and cut into the flour until it is a smooth dough. Add more milk if necessary.

Press the dough into a ball and roll it out on a floured surface. Spread the meat mixture evenly over the dough and roll up, as for a Swiss roll.

Shape the roll into a 'U' shape and cut slits on top. Brush with beaten egg and sprinkle with parsley.

Bake at 220 °C (425 °F, Gas Mark 6) for about 30 minutes or until nicely browned.

JOEY GOOSEN
RUSTENBURG

Spaghetti Bolognaise

Serves 4

45 ml (3 tbsp) olive oil
500 g (1 lb 2 oz) ostrich mince
100 g (3½ oz) bacon, cut in small pieces
1 onion, finely chopped
2 large carrots, finely diced
2 stalks celery, finely diced
1 clove garlic, minced
125 ml (½ cup) fresh chopped parsley
60 ml (4 tbsp) tomato paste
250 ml (9 fl oz) ostrich stock
(see recipe on page 11)
375 ml (13 fl oz) white wine
5 ml (1 tsp) salt
2 ml (½ tsp) each dried oregano, dried thyme,
dried basil and black pepper
1 bay leaf
5 ml (1 tsp) Worcestershire sauce
1 litre (1¾ pints) salted water
250–300 g (9–11 oz) spaghetti
75 ml (5 tbsp) grated Parmesan cheese

Heat the oil in a large frying pan. Fry the mince and bacon thoroughly and drain any excess oil. Add the vegetables and continue to cook until the vegetables are tender. Add the parsley, tomato paste, stock, wine, seasonings and Worcestershire sauce. Reduce heat and simmer for 30 minutes. Discard the bay leaf.

While the sauce simmers, boil the water in a large pot and cook the spaghetti for 9 minutes or until *al dente*. Drain and place on serving plates.

Spoon the sauce over the spaghetti and sprinkle with cheese. Serve immediately.

Source unknown

Chilli Con Carne in Pita Bread

Serves 6

6 pita breads
15 ml (1 tbsp) butter
1 onion, finely chopped
1 stalk celery, diced
400 g (14 oz) ostrich mince
1 x 410 g (14 oz) tin whole tomatoes
60 ml (4 tbsp) tomato sauce
15 ml (1 tbsp) Worcestershire sauce
15 ml (1 tbsp) chilli sauce
5 ml (1 tsp) sugar
1 x 410 g (14 oz) tin red kidney beans

Cut the pitas in half and heat for a few minutes.

Melt the butter in a heavy-based saucepan and add the onion and celery. Cook over medium heat until soft, stirring continuously. Add the mince and cook until brown, stirring all the time. Add crushed tomatoes and remaining ingredients, except the beans. Reduce heat to low and simmer, covered, for 20 minutes. Add beans and reheat.

Serve with your favourite salsa and a sauce made from 125 ml (4½ fl oz) fresh beaten cream, 125 ml (4½ fl oz) mayonnaise and paprika to taste.

RON HENDERSON
MAGALIES OSTRICH RANCH, KROONDAL

Meatloaf à la Peaches

Serves 4–6

Marinade
5 ml (1 tsp) mustard powder
125 ml (½ cup) sugar
30 ml (2 tbsp) vinegar
1 x 725 g (1½ lb) tin peaches, chopped
peach syrup, reserved from tin above

Meatloaf
1 kg (2¼ lb) ostrich mince
250 g (9 oz) ham and bacon, minced
250 ml (1 cup) white breadcrumbs
125 ml (½ cup) grated Cheddar cheese
125 ml (4½ fl oz) milk
2 ml (½ tsp) salt
1 ml (¼ tsp) freshly ground black pepper
250 g (9 oz) cream cheese or
pickled onions to garnish

Mix all the ingredients for the marinade and set aside.

Combine all the ingredients for the meatloaf, except the garnish, mixing well. Mould into a loaf on a piece of foil, close up and bake at 190 °C (375 °F, Gas Mark 4) for 2 hours. After baking for an hour, open up the foil and pour marinade over the meatloaf. Close up the foil and return to the oven. This can be repeated every 15 minutes until cooked.

KLEIN KAROO LANDBOU CO-OPERATIVE

Hamburger Pasty

Serves 6

250 g (9 oz) ready-made dough,
thinly rolled to fit a 23 cm (9 in) pan

Stuffing

1 or 2 large onions, chopped
45 ml (3 tbsp) butter or oil
750 g (1¾ lb) cooked ostrich mince
1 green pepper, chopped
15 ml (1 tbsp) Worcestershire sauce
15 ml (1 tbsp) vinegar or lemon juice
salt and freshly ground black pepper

Top layer

2 eggs, beaten
250 g (9 oz) cream cheese
125 ml (4½ fl oz) cream
2 ml (½ tsp) each nutmeg,
salt and freshly ground black pepper
15 ml (1 tbsp) sugar
paprika

Fry the onions in butter or oil. Add the remaining stuffing ingredients and cook through. Leave to cool, then spread the meat over the dough in the pan.

Mix all the ingredients for the top layer, except the paprika. Pour over the meat and sprinkle with paprika. Cover with dough and bake at 190 °C (375 °F, Gas Mark 4) for 30 minutes or until cooked. Garnish with fresh parsley and stuffed olives and serve hot or cold.

SOURCE UNKNOWN

Ostrich, Pork and Apple Bake

Serves 4–6

500 g (1 lb 2 oz) ostrich mince
500 g (1 lb 2 oz) pork mince
250–500 ml (1–2 cups) breadcrumbs
15 ml (1 tbsp) salt
2 ml (½ tsp) black pepper
2 eggs, beaten
1 ml (¼ tsp) finely crushed cloves
500 g (1 lb 2 oz) cooked noodles
2 large onions, chopped
500 ml (2 cups) chopped, cooked apples
30 ml (2 tbsp) sultanas, chopped
30 ml (2 tbsp) tomato paste,
tomato purée or Italian pasta sauce
60 ml (4 tbsp) grated Cheddar cheese

Mix the meat, breadcrumbs, salt and pepper with the eggs and cloves. Butter a dish and press half the meat into it. Place a thick layer of noodles over the meat, then a layer of onions, apples and sultanas. Mix the leftover meat with the tomato paste and spoon on top of the noodles. Sprinkle with cheese and bake at 180 °C (350 °F, Gas Mark 4) for approximately 30 minutes until cooked and lightly browned.

SOURCE UNKNOWN

Ostrich Pie with Asparagus and Peanuts

Serves 4–6

500 g (1 lb 2 oz) cooked ostrich mince
250 ml (1 cup) ground peanuts
(in food processor or crushed)
7 ml (1½ tsp) salt
375 ml (1½ cups) cooked rice
1 large onion, chopped, fried in butter
3 slices white bread
1 x 410 g (14 oz) tin asparagus salad cuts
flour
500 ml (18 fl oz) milk
butter
30 ml (2 tbsp) cornflour
pinch of cayenne pepper
250 g (9 oz) Cheddar cheese, grated

Mix the mince, peanuts, 5 ml (1 tsp) salt and rice with the fried onions and press into a baking dish. Lay the bread on top and pour the whole tin of asparagus over the bread, juice and all. Make a white sauce with the flour, milk, butter, remaining salt and cayenne pepper and pour over the asparagus. Sprinkle with cheese and bake at 190 °C (375 °F, Gas Mark 4) until brown – about 30–40 minutes.

SOURCE UNKNOWN

Curried Ostrich and Lamb Meatballs

Serves 6

Meatballs
750 g (1¾ lb) ostrich mince
250 g (9 oz) lamb mince
5 slices white bread, soaked in water
2 eggs
nutmeg, cloves, salt and
freshly ground black pepper to taste

Sauce
2–3 onions, chopped
45–60 ml (3–4 tbsp) butter
30 ml (2 tbsp) flour
125 ml (4½ fl oz) vinegar
500 ml (18 fl oz) water
5 ml (1 tsp) turmeric
5 ml (1 tsp) curry powder
30 ml (2 tbsp) apricot jam
30 ml (2 tbsp) sugar
3 or 4 bananas, sliced
salt and freshly ground black pepper

Combine all the ingredients for the meatballs, mould them and fry over medium heat in oil or butter until cooked through. Set to one side, but keep warm.

For the sauce, fry the onions in butter until golden brown. Add flour mixed with vinegar and water. Add turmeric, curry powder, jam, sugar and bananas and cook for a couple of minutes until the bananas are tender. Season to taste.

Place the meatballs in a baking dish, pour over the sauce and bake in moderate oven until heated through.

SOURCE UNKNOWN

Ostrich Ham Rolls

Serves 6

1 kg (2¼ lb) ostrich mince
250 g (9 oz) pork fat, chopped or minced
60 ml (4 tbsp) vinegar or lemon juice
1 egg
30 ml (2 tbsp) dried coriander
2 ml (½ tsp) white pepper
30 ml (2 tbsp) salt
125 ml (½ cup) fine, dried breadcrumbs
30 ml (2 tbsp) sweet white wine (optional)
500 g (1 lb 2 oz) fan fillet, or other large cut of meat
250 g (9 oz) bacon

Mix the mince and fat thoroughly. Add in vinegar, egg and dry ingredients and mix like you would for sausage. Mix in the wine, if desired, then make oblong balls with the mixture. Cut a thin slice of meat from the fillet, season and wrap it around the meatballs. Take a slice of bacon, wrap it around the meat and pin with a toothpick. Place in a pan and bake at 160 °C (325 °F, Gas Mark 3) for 1¼ hours until golden brown.

Use the juices from the pan and add to the following ingredients to make a mustard sauce:

20 ml (4 tsp) mustard powder
20 ml (4 tsp) Worcestershire sauce
45 ml (3 tbsp) butter
125 ml (4½ fl oz) sherry

In a frying pan, add all the ingredients, except the sherry, and bring to the boil. Add the sherry and immediately pour the sauce over the meat rolls. Serve warm.

KLEIN KAROO LANDBOU CO-OPERATIVE

Souzoukaklia

Serves 6

750 g (1¾ lb) ostrich mince
1 medium onion, grated
1 small bunch parsley, finely chopped
2 ml (½ tsp) cayenne pepper
1 ml (¼ tsp) cinnamon
5 ml (1 tsp) allspice
1 ml (¼ tsp) dried coriander
a pinch of ground nutmeg
2 ml (½ tsp) sugar
50 g (1¾ oz) raisins (optional)
salt and freshly ground black pepper to taste
a little oil
lemon wedges to garnish

Combine all the ingredients, except the oil and lemon wedges, and mash to a paste, preferably in an electric mixer or food processor.

Shape the mixture into flattened sausages and arrange on flat, wide-blade skewers. Brush with oil and either grill or barbecue until browned and cooked through.

Slide the meat off the skewers and serve on a bed of rice or in pockets of warm pita breads, garnished with lemon wedges.

SOURCE UNKNOWN

Ostrich Mince Pie with Egg

Serves 6

750 ml (3 cups) cooked ostrich mince
5 ml (1 tsp) nutmeg
30 ml (2 tbsp) vinegar or lemon juice
salt and freshly ground black pepper
1 onion, grated
2 ml (½ tsp) dried thyme
1 ml (¼ tsp) cloves
6 slices ham, chopped
250 g (9 oz) bacon, cooked and chopped
6 hard-boiled eggs, sliced
puff pastry

White sauce
30 ml (2 tbsp) butter
30 ml (2 tbsp) flour
5 ml (1 tsp) salt
500 ml (18 fl oz) milk

Combine all the ingredients except the ham, bacon, eggs and pastry, and mould into small meatballs.

Line a large ovenproof dish with pastry. Place a layer of half of the chopped ham and bacon on top of the pastry, then a layer of meatballs and a layer of egg on top of this. Repeat layers.

To make the sauce, melt the butter and add the flour and salt, stirring until smooth. Slowly pour in the milk, stirring constantly until smooth.

Pour the sauce over the meat and cover with a layer of pastry, pressing down the edges. Bake at 200 °C (400 °F, Gas Mark 6) for 30 minutes. Serve immediately.

SOURCE UNKNOWN

Barbecue

Barbecued Concertina Ostrich Strips

Serves 4–6

500 g (1 lb 2 oz) ostrich fillet steak
20 bamboo skewers

Marinade
30 ml (2 tbsp) soy sauce
20 ml (4 tsp) dry sherry
30 ml (2 tbsp) cooking oil
45 ml (3 tbsp) orange juice
5 ml (1 tsp) grated orange rind
10 ml (2 tsp) chopped root ginger
salt and freshly ground black pepper to taste

Wrap the meat lightly in cling wrap and set it in the freezer for 30 minutes until partially frozen. In the meantime, soak the bamboo skewers in hot water for 30 minutes.

Cut the fillet into paper-thin strips and thread concertina-style onto the bamboo skewers. Mix all the marinade ingredients in a glass bowl and marinate the meat in it for 4 hours or overnight.

Grill the meat very slowly over coals until cooked, basting occasionally with the remaining marinade. (Do not overcook the meat or it will become tough.)

Serve immediately.

SOURCE UNKNOWN

Ostrich Barbecued Meat with Mint

Serves 6

10 ml (2 tsp) salt
pepper to taste
10 ml (2 tsp) mustard powder
6 cuts of ostrich fillet, well tenderised
125 ml (4½ fl oz) vinegar, lemon juice or white wine
1 clove garlic, crushed
5 ml (1 tsp) grated lemon rind
30 ml (2 tbsp) freshly ground mint leaves
125 ml (4½ fl oz) oil
10 ml (2 tsp) sugar

Mix the salt, pepper and mustard and rub it into the meat. Place in a dish and set aside. Mix the vinegar, garlic, lemon rind, mint, oil and sugar (the marinade) and pour over the meat 4 hours prior to your barbecue. Turn regularly.

You can grill the meat in an oven under the grill, turning once and pouring over the remaining marinade, or you can barbecue the meat on an open fire like you would a normal beef fillet, brushing regularly with marinade.

SOURCE UNKNOWN

Lemon and Herb Fan Fillets

Serves 4

juice of 2 lemons
5 ml (1 tsp) garlic, lemon and parsley seasoning
pinch of mixed herbs
30 ml (2 tbsp) olive oil
4 fan fillets (about 200 g/7 oz each)

Combine the lemon juice, seasoning, herbs and oil and marinate the fillets overnight in the refrigerator.

Seal the meat on both sides in a hot pan or over hot coals, basting with the marinade. Do not overcook (approximate cooking time – 4 minutes on each side).

For a light meal, the cooked fillet can be thinly sliced and served on fresh bread rolls.

CHRIS PATON
PRETORIA

Ostrich Potjie

Serves 4

1 kg (2¼ lb) ostrich steak, cut into cubes
75 ml (5 tbsp) oil
3 large onions, coarsely chopped
2 cloves garlic, crushed
500 g (1 lb 2 oz) baby carrots
1 punnet patty pans
1 punnet baby marrows
1 punnet mushrooms
1 packet powdered vegetable soup
500 ml (2 cups) grated cheese
250 ml (9 fl oz) wine
250 ml (9 fl oz) water
seasoning to taste
(bear in mind that the soup already has some salt in it)

In the pot, braise the meat in the oil. Add the onions and garlic and mix well. Place the vegetables in a layer on top of the meat and sprinkle with the soup powder. Add the wine to moisten it (if this quantity isn't sufficient, add the water). Close the pot and simmer over a low fire for about 2 hours. Add water as necessary, but do not stir.

When the ingredients are cooked, cover with cheese and cook for another 15 minutes or until the cheese has melted. Add seasoning 5–10 minutes before the end of the cooking time.

CHRIS PATON
PRETORIA

Ostrich Stir-fry (page 94)

Honey-glazed Ostrich Shish-Kebabs (page 81)

Honey-glazed Ostrich Shish-Kebabs

Serves 12

Marinade
250 ml (9 fl oz) red wine
1 onion, thinly sliced
15 ml (1 tbsp) dried rosemary
5 ml (1 tsp) dried thyme
4–5 cloves garlic, crushed
180 ml (6¼ fl oz) olive oil
5 ml (1 tsp) chopped parsley
10 ml (2 tsp) white pepper
45 ml (3 tbsp) Worcestershire sauce
3–4 bay leaves

4 kg (8¾ lb) ostrich steak or fillet, cut into cubes
2 tomatoes, cut into cubes
2 onions, cut into cubes
1 green pepper, cut into cubes
125 ml (4½ fl oz) honey, warmed

Combine the marinade ingredients in a glass or ceramic container. Place the meat in the marinade, cover the bowl and leave in the refrigerator for 24 hours.

Skewer, alternating the meat and vegetables. Suspend the skewers over a shallow pan and baste with honey, allowing excess to run off.

Cook over medium fire on a covered grill, turning once – total cooking time about 10 minutes. Do not overcook.

CHRIS PATON
PRETORIA

Cowboy Steaks with Tangy Sauce

Serves 6

Sauce
1 onion, chopped
2 cloves garlic, crushed
2 stalks celery, chopped
15 ml (1 tbsp) cake flour
30 ml (2 tbsp) soy sauce
1 x 340 ml (12 fl oz) can beer
45 ml (3 tbsp) chilli sauce, or less to taste
15 ml (1 tbsp) prepared mustard
2 ml (½ tsp) Tabasco sauce

6 ostrich steaks, 25 mm (1 in) thick
salt and freshly ground black pepper to taste

Prepare the sauce by mixing all ingredients and simmer for 30 minutes. Set aside and leave to cool.

Grill the steaks over hot coals, basting regularly with the sauce – rare takes 5–7 minutes per side, medium takes 7–10 minutes per side. Season. Heat remaining sauce and serve immediately with the steaks.

SOURCE UNKNOWN

NOTE – OSTRICH SHOULD NEVER BE COOKED TO WELL DONE. IT WILL BE VERY DRY.

Ostrich All-in-One Pot

Serves 6–8

750 g (1¾ lb) ostrich goulash
1 pig's trotter, sawn into 15 mm (⅝ in) thick slices
25 ml (5 tsp) cooking oil
2 onions, sliced
salt and freshly ground black pepper to taste
2 ml (½ tsp) dried or
10 ml (2 tsp) chopped fresh thyme
200 g (7 oz) uncooked pearl wheat,
soaked overnight in 750 ml (1¼ pints) water
4 tomatoes, skinned and chopped
250 ml (9 fl oz) dry white wine, heated
250 ml (9 fl oz) meat stock, heated
45 ml (3 tbsp) fruit chutney, heated
2 leeks, sliced
10 baby marrows, halved
10 carrots, quartered

Brown the ostrich and pig's trotter in heated oil in a three-legged pot. Add the onions and sauté until translucent. Season with salt, pepper and thyme and add the pearl wheat and tomatoes. In a separate saucepan, combine the wine, stock and chutney and heat through. Pour the liquid into the large pot and simmer for 2–2½ hours over moderate to cool coals or until the meat is almost tender. Layer the vegetables on top and simmer for 15–20 minutes until cooked but still crisp.

KLEIN KAROO LANDBOU CO-OPERATIVE

VARIATION: Substitute 1 kg (2¼ lb) ostrich neck for the goulash.

Barbecued Ostrich

Serves 6

6 x135 g (4¾ oz) ostrich fillets
10 ml (2 tsp) salt
freshly ground black pepper
10 ml (2 tsp) mustard powder
1 clove garlic, crushed
125 ml (4½ fl oz) vinegar
60 ml (4 tbsp) lemon juice
15 ml (1 tbsp) grated lemon rind
5–10 ml (1–2 tsp) artificial sweetener
30 ml (2 tbsp) oil

Mix the salt, pepper and mustard in a bowl. Rub the mixture into the fillets and place the meat in a dish.

Combine the garlic, vinegar, lemon juice, lemon rind, sweetener and oil in a separate bowl and mix well. Pour over steaks and leave to marinate for 1 hour.

Remove the steaks, reserving the marinade for basting, and barbecue the fillets for about 4 minutes on each side, basting frequently. Serve immediately.

WEIGHLESS MAGAZINE

Ostrich Fillet on the Barbecue

Serves 4–6

3 cloves garlic, chopped
1 ostrich fillet
250 ml (9 fl oz) cream
2 lemons, juiced and rind grated
2 bay leaves
salt and freshly ground black pepper to taste
5 ml (1 tsp) black peppercorns

Stuff the chopped garlic into the fillet and marinate with the remaining ingredients overnight.

Place on a very hot barbecue for 5 minutes on each side to seal. Cook over medium fire until done. While cooking, baste frequently with the marinade.

DANELLE COULSON
HEKPOORT

Whole Ostrich Leg/Buttock on a Spit

Serves 30

1 ostrich leg/buttock
1 whole garlic
500 g (1 lb 2 oz) streaky bacon

Marinade/Basting sauce
1.25 litres (2¼ pints) lemon juice
4 green peppers, finely grated
15 ml (1 tbsp) black peppercorns, crushed
2 bay leaves
375 g (13 oz) apricot jam
750 ml (1¼ pints) oil
750 ml (1¼ pints) red wine
seasoning to taste
30 ml (2 tbsp) mixed herbs
90 ml (6 tbsp) garlic flakes
90 ml (6 tbsp) chicken marinade

Prepare the marinade 24 hours in advance by combining all the ingredients. Make holes on all sides of the meat and stuff with garlic and bacon. Inject 500 ml (18 fl oz) of the marinate into the meat.

On a spit, the meat will take approximately 6 hours for medium rare, and 8–10 hours for medium well. The fire must be very hot for the first 30 minutes to seal the meat, reduce heat for the rest of the cooking period.

DANELLE COULSON
HEKPOORT

Other marinades to try with this recipe:
   * Lemon juice, oil, herbs of your choice, white wine and seasoning to taste.
   * The same as above, but with fresh chillies to taste.

Ostrich Carpet Bag Steak

Serves 4

1 kg (2¼ lb) ostrich steak,
cut into 4 slices about 35 mm (1½ in) thick
16 fresh oysters
1 fresh lemon
freshly ground black pepper
25 ml (5 tsp) butter
salt to taste
5 ml (1 tsp) chopped parsley

Cut a pocket into each of the steaks and fill each with 4 oysters. Sprinkle with a few drops of lemon juice and dust with pepper. Secure with poultry pins or sew up the pockets with fine string and a trussing needle. Brush with a little melted butter and barbecue for 6–10 minutes on each side.

Just before the steaks are done, melt the remaining butter in a small pan and, when it is brown, squeeze in the rest of the lemon juice and season with salt and pepper and chopped parsley.

Pour the bubbling butter over the steaks and serve.

PAULINE HENDERSON
MAGALIES OSTRICH RANCH, KROONDAL

Ostrich-neck Pot

Serves 10

2 large onions, chopped
3 kg (6½ lb) ostrich neck, cut into portions
½ packet pepper steak marinade
2 kg (4½ lb) small sweet potatoes
30 ml (2 tbsp) mixed spices
15 ml (1 tbsp) freshly ground black pepper
salt to taste
100 g (3½ oz) mushrooms
45 ml (3 tbsp) butter
2 lemons, squeezed and juice reserved

Fry the onions in a little fat or oil and add the meat. Stir to coat and simmer with the lid on for about 1½ hours.

Mix the marinade according to the instructions on the packet and add it to the meat, together with the sweet potatoes. Simmer for 1 hour, then add the mixed spices and pepper. Check for salt.

While the main dish is simmering, chop the mushrooms and fry them in melted butter. Stir in the lemon juice and serve as a side dish with the ostrich pot.

JOOD VAN JUYSSTEEN
STAMPRIET

Curried Ostrich Steak Potjie

Serves 10

3 kg (6½ lb) ostrich steak or fillet, cut into cubes
4 carrots, sliced
4 turnips, diced
2 onions, chopped
60 ml (4 tbsp) soy sauce
20 ml (4 tsp) curry powder (or to taste)
125 g (4½ oz) mango chutney
225 g (8 oz) peach chutney
15 ml (1 tbsp) turmeric
10 ml (2 tsp) mixed herbs
salt to taste
5 ml (1 tsp) freshly ground black pepper
125 ml (½ cup) grated Cheddar cheese
1 pawpaw, sliced
4 bananas, sliced
125 ml (½ cup) desiccated coconut
125 ml (½ cup) peanuts, chopped

Place the cubes of meat in the potjie and add the carrots, turnips and onions. Pour over the soy sauce and add enough water to cover the meat and vegetables. Simmer for approximately 1 hour.

Mix the curry powder, chutneys, turmeric, herbs, salt, pepper and cheese and add to the potjie. Simmer to allow the flavourings to permeate, then serve on boiled rice with pawpaw, bananas, coconut and peanuts.

SOURCE UNKNOWN

Ostrich Biltong and Pumpkin Potjie

Serves 8–12

1 kg (2¼ lb) bacon, sliced
3 kg (6½ lb) ostrich biltong (preferably moist),
cut into thick slices
1 kg (2¼ lb) stoned prunes
500 g (1 lb 2 oz) rice
2 kg (4½ lb) pumpkin, peeled and sliced
1 beef stock cube
250 ml (9 fl oz) soy sauce
250 ml (1 cup) grated Cheddar cheese

Fry the bacon in the potjie until crisp, then add the biltong slices and prunes. Pack in the rice and then the pumpkin on top. Make up the stock and mix it with the soy sauce. Add to the potjie. Leave to simmer gently until the rice and pumpkin are cooked. Sprinkle cheese on top and allow to melt. Serve immediately.

SOURCE UNKNOWN

Ostrich Fillet with Liqueur Sauce

Serves 10

2 kg (4½ lb) ostrich fillet, sliced
250 ml (9 fl oz) soy sauce
1 x 410 g 14 oz) tin mushroom soup
½ packet pepperoni salad dressing
(mixed according to packet instructions)
10 button mushrooms, chopped
375 ml (13 fl oz) of your favourite liqueur,
or sweet or red wine
250 ml (1 cup) peach chutney
500 g (1 lb 2 oz) rice
125 g (4½ oz) butter
1 green pumpkin, peeled and sliced
10 ml (2 tsp) ground cinnamon
125 ml (½ cup) sugar
salt to taste

Spread a little soy sauce over the meat and barbecue until only half done. Combine the remaining soy sauce, mushroom soup, salad dressing, mushrooms, wine and chutney. Heat the sauce.

Dip the meat in the warm sauce and barbeque quickly for a few seconds. Place the meat back in the sauce and serve from this dish, together with rice that has been cooked separately in salted water.

Pumpkin
Melt the butter in a pot and add the pumpkin slices (pack some lumps of butter on top of the pumpkin). Sprinkle with cinnamon, sugar and a little salt. Simmer slowly for about 45 minutes.

SOURCE UNKNOWN

Lighter Meals

Ostrich Liver and Bacon Kebabs

Serves 4

300 g (11 oz) ostrich liver, cut into 5 cm (2 in) cubes
6 rashers rindless streaky bacon, halved and rolled up
3 medium onions, quartered, or 12 small onions
12 button mushrooms
oil for brushing
5 ml (1 tsp) salt
2 ml (½ tsp) pepper

Preheat the grill to 180 °C (350 °F, Gas Mark 4). Thread the liver, bacon, onion and mushrooms alternately onto 4 metal skewers. Place the skewers in the grill pan. Brush with oil and sprinkle with salt and pepper. Place under the grill for 10 minutes, turning often and basting now and then with the pan juices. Serve immediately.

DANELLE COULSON
HEKPOORT

Fried Ostrich Liver and Onions

Serves 4

750 g (1¾ lb) ostrich liver
4 large onions, sliced into rings
25 ml (5 tsp) butter
salt and freshly ground black pepper

Melt the butter in a large, heavy-based skillet. Add the liver and fry over medium heat until almost done. Remove meat and set aside. Add the onion to the pan and fry until translucent. Return the meat to the pan and cook for 5 or 6 minutes until the liver is cooked and the onions are starting to brown. Season. Serve immediately.

KLEIN KAROO LANDBOU CO-OPERATIVE

Teriyaki Ostrich Wings

Serves 4

125 ml (4½ fl oz) water
200 ml (7 fl oz) soy sauce
2 cloves garlic, minced
5 ml (1 tsp) ground ginger
15 ml (1 tbsp) brown sugar
4 ostrich wings, washed and patted dry
with paper towels

Combine all the ingredients, except the wings, and mix thoroughly. Marinate the wings in the sauce overnight.

Preheat oven to 180 °C (350 °F, Gas Mark 4). Remove wings from the sauce and place in a baking dish. Brush with sauce and roast, uncovered, for 45 minutes (or until wings are done), basting frequently with remaining sauce.

KLEIN KAROO LANDBOU CO-OPERATIVE

Peri-Peri Ostrich Wings

Serves 4

Sauce
1 x 65 g (2¼ oz) tin tomato paste
2 cloves garlic, crushed
1 onion, grated
45 ml (3 tbsp) brown sugar
2–5 ml (½–1 tsp) peri-peri powder (or to taste)
350 ml (12 fl oz) beef stock
20 ml (4 tsp) butter
20 ml (4 tsp) cornflour mixed with
30 ml (2 tbsp) cold water

salt and freshly ground black pepper
4 ostrich wings, washed and patted dry
with paper towels
30 ml (2 tbsp) butter, melted
4 cloves garlic, crushed

Place all the sauce ingredients in a pot and cook until thickened – about 5 minutes.

Season the wings and place on a baking tray. Brush with melted butter and crushed garlic and then the sauce. Grill under a very hot grill, turning once to ensure that both sides are well cooked and browned. Remove from the oven and add the remaining sauce. Garnish with parsley.

ORIENT BUTCHERY
MAGALIESBURG

Hot Texas Ostrich Wings

Serves 4

4 ostrich wings, washed and patted dry
with paper towels
125 ml (4½ fl oz) chilli sauce
45 ml (3 tbsp) soy sauce
2 cloves garlic, minced
2 ml (½ tsp) cayenne pepper
2 ml (½ tsp) freshly ground black pepper
60 ml (4 tbsp) brown sugar

Place the wings in a casserole dish and cover with foil. Bake in a preheated oven at 180 °C (350 °F, Gas Mark 4) for 45 minutes.

While the wings are baking, blend the remaining ingredients together. Uncover the wings and pour over the sauce. Re-cover and bake for 45 minutes until the wings are tender. Serve immediately.

AMERICAN OSTRICH ASSOCIATION

Honey and Garlic Ostrich Wings

As a variation, follow the previous method to prepare the wings, but blend 1 litre (1¾ pints) sunflower oil, 250 ml (9 fl oz) liquid honey and 15 ml (1 tbsp) garlic powder in place of the hot Texas sauce.

Ostrich Biltong

For each 25 kg (55 lb) of meat:

5 litres (9 pints) vinegar
1.25 kg (2¾ lb) good-quality, fine salt
250 ml (1 cup) brown sugar
45 ml (3 tbsp) bicarbonate of soda
20 ml (4 tsp) potassium nitrate (saltpetre) (optional)
25 ml (5 tsp) pepper
100 g (3½ oz) coarsely ground coriander

Cut the meat into strips 5–7 cm thick. Immerse the strips in vinegar and leave for a few minutes.

Mix the remaining ingredients and rub the mixture into the meat. Layer the meat, larger pieces at the bottom, in a wooden, earthenware, plastic or enamel container – never use a metal container because the salt may cause a reaction. Sprinkle a little vinegar over each layer. Leave in a cool place for 24–48 hours, depending on how thick the meat is and how salty you want it to be.

Dip the biltong in a mixture of 45 ml (3 tbsp) vinegar and 5 litres (8¾ pints) warm water.

Dry the pieces and hang them on S-shaped hooks or pieces of string so that the air can circulate freely around them. Protect the meat from flies and dust. Leave for about 2–3 weeks, depending on how tender the meat is.

KLEIN KAROO LANDBOU CO-OPERATIVE

Droë Wors (Dried Sausage)

Makes approximately 3.5 kg (7½ lb)

3 kg (6½ lb) ostrich mince
500 g (1 lb 2 oz) mutton tail fat
20 ml (4 tsp) salt
2 ml (½ tsp) pepper
45 ml (3 tbsp) ground roasted coriander
2 ml (½ tsp) ground allspice
2 ml (½ tsp) ground cloves
25 ml (5 tsp) vinegar
85 g (3 oz) sausage casing

Mince all the ingredients together coarsely and fill the sausage casing loosely with the mixture. Hang up to dry in a cold, dry place, making sure that the sausages are protected from flies and dust.

KLEIN KAROO LANDBOU CO-OPERATIVE

Boerewors (Farm-style Sausage)

Serves 6

45 ml (3 tbsp) dried coriander
2 ml (½ tsp) nutmeg
1 ml (¼ tsp) ground cloves
2 ml (½ tsp) ground dried thyme
2 ml (½ tsp) ground allspice
25 ml (5 tsp) salt
5 ml (1 tsp) pepper
1.5 kg (3¼ lb) ostrich mince
1.5 kg (3¼ lb) pork, lamb or venison mince
500 g (1 lb 2 oz) pork belly fat,
cut into 6 mm (¼ in) cubes
125 ml (4½ fl oz) vinegar
1 clove garlic, crushed
45 ml (3 tbsp) Worcestershire sauce
85 g (3 oz) sausage casing

Roast the coriander until light brown, then grind and mix it with all the spices and salt and pepper. Mince the meat coarsely and mix very lightly with all the other ingredients. Fill the casings not too firmly with the meat mixture. Do not knead the meat, otherwise the sausage will be too firm. Also ensure that the cubes of pork fat are evenly distributed.

SARAH STEYN
HEKPOORT

Ostrich Steak and Mushroom Crêpes

Serves 6

45 ml (3 tbsp) oil
450 g (1 lb) ostrich steaks,
cut into 6 mm (¼ in) thick strips
80 g (2¾ oz) mushrooms, sliced
30 ml (2 tbsp) butter
30 ml (2 tbsp) flour
250 ml (9 fl oz) milk
1 ml (¼ tsp) salt
1 ml (¼ tsp) white pepper
pinch of nutmeg
12 crêpes (see recipe in on page 126)

Heat the oil in a large skillet and quickly fry the steak and mushrooms. Set aside.

In a separate pot, melt the butter. Remove from heat and blend in the flour. Slowly add the milk, salt, pepper and nutmeg. Cook until thickened.

Add the cream sauce to the steak and mushrooms, spoon the mixture onto the warmed crêpes, roll up and serve immediately.

SOURCE UNKNOWN

Ostrich Liver in Red Wine Sauce

Serves 4

2–3 onions, sliced
2 cloves garlic, minced
30 ml (2 tbsp) butter or oil
5 ml (1 tsp) sugar
salt and freshly ground black pepper to taste
750 g (1¾ lb) ostrich liver, cut into cubes
flour to coat the cubes of liver
250 g (9 oz) lean bacon
1 bay leaf
250 ml (9 fl oz) red wine

Fry the onions and garlic with the sugar in butter until yellow. Sprinkle salt and pepper over the liver, roll it in flour and brown on all sides. Lace an ovenproof dish with half the bacon and a layer of onions. Place the liver on top and cover with the rest of the onions and bacon and the bay leaf. (The bacon must be lean or the dish will be very fatty.) Pour the wine over and bake at 190 °C (375 °F, Gas Mark 4) for about 45 minutes until tender.

SOURCE UNKNOWN

Ostrich Liver with Citrus and Peppercorn Sauce

Serves 6

750 g (1¾ lb) ostrich liver, sliced
75 ml (5 tbsp) flour
180 g (6½ oz) butter
125 ml (½ cup) fine sugar
3 oranges
2 grapefruits
15 ml (1 tbsp) green peppercorns

Dust the slices of liver with flour.

In a skillet, heat 80 g (2¾ oz) of the butter and sauté the liver for 3 minutes per side.

To prepare the sauce, heat the remaining butter in a saucepan. Add the sugar and caramelize it. Add the juice from 2 oranges and 1 grapefruit. Zest the remaining orange and grapefruit, then section each. Add 10 ml (2 tsp) of orange zest and 5 ml (1 tsp) of grapefruit zest to the sauce. Cook for 1 minute. Remove from heat and add the fruit sections and peppercorns.

Place the sautéed liver on serving plates, cover with sauce and serve.

SOURCE UNKNOWN

Ostrich Meat Cakes

Serves 6

500 ml (2 cups) cooked ostrich mince
250 ml (1 cup) mashed potato
15 ml (1 tbsp) chopped parsley
1 egg, lightly beaten
salt and pepper to taste
oil for frying
extra chopped parsley

Mix the mince with the remaining ingredients. Make small patties and fry in hot oil. Roll in chopped parsley.

SOURCE UNKNOWN

Ostrich Stir-fry

Serves 4

600 g (1 ¼ lb) ostrich fillet or steak, thinly sliced
100 ml (3 ½ fl oz) soy sauce
5 ml (1 tsp) garlic, lemon and parsley seasoning
2 medium onions, thinly sliced
2 sweet peppers of different colours, thinly sliced
30 ml (2 tbsp) oil

Marinate meat with soy sauce and seasoning, cover and place in the refrigerator for 12 hours. Braise the onions and peppers in oil over low heat, covered, until soft. Turn up the heat and add meat, cooking until brown. Add a little water if it becomes too dry. Check seasoning.
Serve on rice or macaroni with a fresh green salad.

SOURCE UNKNOWN

Ostrich Liver Loaf with Brown Onion Sauce

Serves 3–4

Onion sauce

2 onions, grated
30 ml (2 tbsp) oil
30 ml (2 tbsp) gravy powder
375 ml (13 fl oz) cold water

Meatloaf

15 ml (1 tbsp) finely chopped onions
30 ml (2 tbsp) butter
500 g (1 lb 2 oz) ostrich liver
250 ml (1 cup) fresh white breadcrumbs
2 eggs
60 ml (4 tbsp) meat extract (beef cubes)
60 ml (4 tbsp) milk
2 ml (½ tsp) salt to taste
1 ml (¼ tsp) pepper
15 ml (1 tbsp) fine parsley
1 ml (¼ tsp) ground cloves

For the sauce, fry the onions in oil and stir in the gravy powder. Slowly add cold water and seasoning. Simmer until the sauce thickens and is heated through.

To make the loaf, fry the onions in butter. Mince the liver and add the remaining ingredients – gradually add the liquid to prevent the mixture from becoming too sloppy. Mould a loaf and place it in a baking dish. Bake at 190 °C (375 °F, Gas Mark 4) for about 20–30 minutes until done.

Turn out the loaf onto a serving dish and pour onion gravy over. Serve with curried beans or sliced boiled egg and tomato.

KLEIN KAROO LANDBOU CO-OPERATIVE

Ostrich Mince Croquettes

Serves 4

30 ml (2 tbsp) butter
60 ml (4 tbsp) flour
250 ml (9 fl oz) milk
500 ml (2 cups) cooked ostrich mince
2 ml (½ tsp) each salt, paprika and chilli powder
1 ml (¼ tsp) pepper
5 ml (1 tsp) Worcestershire sauce
10 ml (2 tsp) soy sauce
5 ml (1 tsp) finely chopped parsley
1 egg
30 ml (2 tbsp) water
125 ml (½ cup) seasoned flour
375 ml (1½ cups) fine breadcrumbs
250 ml (9 fl oz) sunflower oil

Heat the butter in a saucepan. Add the flour and cook over low heat for 2 minutes. Slowly stir in the milk and simmer into a very thick sauce. Stirring constantly, add the mince, seasonings, Worcestershire sauce, soy sauce and parsley. Cool to room temperature and then shape the mixture into equally sized patties.

Blend the egg with the water, dust each patty with seasoned flour, dip into the egg mixture and then coat with breadcrumbs.

Heat the oil in a large skillet and fry the patties to a golden brown on each side. Serve immediately.

PAULINE HENDERSON
MAGALIES OSTRICH RANCH, KROONDAL

Ostrich, Bacon and Smoked Mussel Fry (page 114)

Ostrich Steak Tartare (page 67)

Ostrich Hamburgers

Serves 4

Burgers
750 g (1¾ lb) ostrich mince
1 egg
30 ml (2 tbsp) fine breadcrumbs
30 ml (2 tbsp) minced onion
15 ml (1 tbsp) Dijon mustard
5 ml (1 tsp) Worcestershire sauce

Sauce
45 ml (3 tbsp) oil
60 ml (4 tbsp) minced onion
60 ml (4 tbsp) minced green pepper
60 ml (4 tbsp) minced celery
750 ml (3 cups) chopped tomatoes
15 ml (1 tbsp) salt
45 ml (3 tbsp) wine vinegar
2 ml (½ tsp) hot mustard powder
90 ml (6 tbsp) tomato paste
2 ml (½ tsp) each dried basil, dried thyme,
dried oregano, paprika, garlic powder and pepper
90 ml (6 tbsp) brown sugar

To make the burgers, place all the ingredients in a large mixing bowl and blend thoroughly. Form into patties and place on a baking sheet lined with wax paper. Cover with another layer of wax paper and refrigerate until needed.

To prepare the sauce, heat the oil in a saucepan, add the vegetables and sauté until tender. Add the remaining ingredients, reduce heat and simmer until the liquid is reduced by two-thirds.

Grill or fry the burgers over medium heat, frequently brushing with sauce. Serve hot with extra sauce on the hamburger buns.

AMERICAN OSTRICH ASSOCIATION

Mini Ostrich Burgers

Serves 8

2 spring onions
400 g (14 oz) ostrich mince
1 egg
30 ml (2 tbsp) olive oil
salt and freshly ground black pepper
flour

Finely slice the spring onions and mix with the mince, egg, olive oil and seasoning. Form into small patties – about 15 ml (1 tbsp) of mixture for each patty. Dust with flour and fry in a dash of olive oil, leaving the patties pink in the centre.

Serve on fried bread or mini burger buns topped with mayonnaise and lettuce. Finish with a twist of red pepper as garnish.

THE AUSTRALIAN OSTRICH COMPANY

Ostrich Meat and Vegetable Pie

Serves 4

60 ml (4 tbsp) butter
60 ml (4 tbsp) flour
2 ml (½ tsp) salt
500 ml (18 fl oz) milk
500 ml (2 cups) cooked or canned mixed vegetables
1 ml (¼ tsp) cayenne pepper
2 ml (½ tsp) nutmeg
500 ml (2 cups) cubed, cooked ostrich steak or fillet
250 g (9 oz) Cheddar cheese, grated
300 g (11 oz) cooked mashed potato

Make a sauce by melting the butter and adding the flour and salt, stirring until smooth, then slowly adding the milk, stirring continuously. Add the vegetables, salt to taste, cayenne pepper, nutmeg and meat. Fold in the cheese.

Place in a greased ovenproof dish and cover with mashed potato. Bake at 200 °C (400 °F, Gas Mark 6) for 20 minutes.

KLEIN KAROO LANDBOU CO-OPERATIVE

Ostrich and Asparagus Quiche

Serves 8

Crust
250 ml (1 cup) flour
250 ml (1 cup) grated Cheddar cheese
10 ml (2 tsp) grated Parmesan cheese
salt and freshly ground black pepper
a pinch of cayenne pepper

Filling
1 ostrich neck
1 bunch chives, sliced
2 onions, chopped
200 g (7 oz) bacon, chopped
200 g (7 oz) leeks, washed and sliced
25 ml (5 tsp) butter
15 ml (1 tbsp) oil
4 slices ham, diced
300 g (11 oz) asparagus salad cuts, drained
25 ml (5 tsp) tomato sauce
250 ml (1 cup) grated Cheddar cheese
4 eggs
15 ml (1 tbsp) flour
500 ml (18 fl oz) cream
salt and freshly ground black pepper to taste
a pinch each nutmeg and cayenne pepper

Cook the ostrich neck until tender. When cool, strip the meat from the bones and cut into cubes. Set aside 500 ml (2 cups) of meat and discard the bones.

For the crust, blend the flour, cheeses and seasonings. Press the pastry into a large pie dish, covering the base and sides. Prick the pastry with a fork and sprinkle 45 ml (3 tbsp) chives over the pastry base. Allow to rest in the refrigerator while preparing the filling.

To make the filling, fry the onions, bacon and leeks in butter and oil, then add the balance of chives and fry lightly. Remove from heat, add the ham and ostrich and combine well. Place half of this mixture over the chives, spread asparagus cuts evenly over the top and cover with the balance of the meat mixture. Dot with tomato sauce, then sprinkle with cheese.

Beat the eggs and flour together, then add the cream, seasoning, nutmeg and cayenne pepper and pour over the cheese. Bake at 180 °C (350 °F, Gas Mark 4) in a preheated oven for 30–40 minutes.

ORIENT BUTCHERY
MAGALIESBURG

Ostrich Schnitzels

Serves 6

6 thinly sliced ostrich steaks
(1 cm/⅜ in thick, hand-sized)
salt and freshly ground black pepper
flour
3 eggs, beaten
cornflake crumbs

Tenderise the steaks by beating them with a wooden meat mallet, and season with salt and pepper. Dip the steaks in flour, making sure that they are well covered. Dip steaks in beaten egg and cover with crumbs.

Place the schnitzels in the refrigerator to 'rest' for at least 4 hours. The schnitzels can then be fried in hot oil or frozen until required. If freezing, place a piece of cling wrap or wax paper between each schnitzel.

For a perfect German schnitzel meal, serve with potato salad, hot sauerkraut, a few slices of tomato, sweet-and-sour gherkins and lettuce. A fresh cucumber or banana salad would complement the meal.

GRETCHEN MEYER
KROONDAL

Szechwan Shredded Ostrich Steak

Serves 6

Marinade
45 ml (3 tbsp) sherry
45 ml (3 tbsp) soy sauce
5 ml (1 tsp) minced garlic
5 ml (1 tsp) minced ginger
2 ml (½ tsp) cayenne pepper

30 ml (2 tbsp) olive oil
750 g (1¾ lb) ostrich steak, very thinly sliced

Blend the marinade ingredients, pour over the steak and mix through. Marinate for 30 minutes.

Heat the oil to very hot in a wok or large skillet and add the undrained steak.

Stir-fry for 5 minutes and serve immediately on a bed of noodles.

PAULINE HENDERSON
MAGALIES OSTRICH RANCH, KROONDAL

Ostrich Liver and Kidney Pie

Serves 6

Pastry
120 g (4 oz) cake flour
a pinch of salt
50 g (1¾ oz) lard
ice water
10 ml (2 tsp) mampoer (or Stroh rum)

Sauce
15 ml (1 tbsp) tomato purée
125 ml (4½ fl oz) beef stock
2 cloves
15 ml (1 tbsp) water
15 ml (1 tbsp) sugar
salt and freshly ground black pepper to taste
125 ml (4½ fl oz) milk
15 ml (1 tbsp) cornflour

Filling
30 ml (2 tbsp) lard
5 ml (1 tsp) grated lemon peel
1 onion, grated
1 carrot, finely grated
500 g (1 lb 2 oz) ostrich kidney, diced
500 g (1 lb 2 oz) ostrich liver, diced
15 ml (1 tbsp) lemon juice
30 ml (2 tbsp) breadcrumbs

To make the pastry, sift the flour and salt twice. Finely shred the lard and add it to the flour. Mix to a firm dough with the water and mampoer. Roll out half the dough and line a pie dish about 23 cm (9 in) in diameter. Store in the refrigerator with the rest of the dough.

To prepare the sauce, boil all the ingredients, except the milk and cornflour, for about 3 minutes. Add the milk and cornflour to thicken the sauce. Keep warm until ready to serve with the pie.

To make the filling, fry the fat, lemon peel, onion and carrot until lightly browned. Add the kidney, liver and lemon juice and fry. Cover and simmer until tender – approximately 45 minutes. Thicken the gravy with the breadcrumbs. Spoon the mixture into the prepared pastry dish. Roll out the remaining pastry and lay it over the top, pressing to seal the edges. Bake at 190 °C (375 °F, Gas Mark 4) until golden brown – about 25 minutes. Serve with the sauce.

SOURCE UNKNOWN

Mushroom and Ostrich-neck Pie

Serves 6

1 ostrich neck, sliced
250 g (9 oz) pork fat or fatty meat
15 ml (1 tbsp) salt and freshly ground black pepper
125 ml (4½ fl oz) vinegar
5 ml (1 tsp) peppercorns
1 ml (¼ tsp) nutmeg
1 x 410 g (14 oz) tin mushroom soup

good-quality pastry for top and bottom of pie

Cover the meat with water and add all the remaining ingredients, except the nutmeg and soup. Simmer for about 3–4 hours until the meat is tender and comes off the bone. Remove the bones – be careful of fine bones in the neck – and mash the meat finely. Add the nutmeg and soup and cook for 15 minutes. The meat must be of a tender 'soupy' consistency, not dry.

Line a pie dish with pastry, spoon the meat mixture over it and cover with another layer of pastry. Brush the pastry with egg if desired and bake at 180 °C (350 °F, Gas Mark 4) for about 15–20 minutes until brown.

KELIN KAROO LANDBOU CO-OPERATIVE

Ostrich Pie (1)

Serves 6

25 ml (5 tsp) olive oil
150 g (5½ oz) pork fat, diced
1 kg (2¼ lb) ostrich steak, cut into cubes
1 large onion, finely chopped
2 stalks celery, finely chopped
25 ml (5 tsp) lemon juice
10 ml (2 tsp) salt
250 ml (9 fl oz) boiling water
3 bay leaves
10 black peppercorns
6 whole cloves
45 ml (3 tbsp) port or any dessert wine
ready-made pastry

Heat the oil in a heavy-based saucepan and brown the fat. Add the ostrich and brown, then add the onion, celery, lemon juice, salt and water. Place the bay leaves, peppercorns and cloves in a muslin bag and add to the saucepan. Add the port and simmer gently until the meat falls apart.

Line a pie dish with pastry, spoon in the mixture to cover the base and place another layer of pastry on top. Bake in a preheated oven at 180 °C (350 °F, Gas Mark 4) for 15 minutes or until the crust is crispy. Serve immediately.

SOURCE UNKNOWN

Ostrich Pie (2)

Serves 4

Filling
500 g (1 lb 2 oz) ostrich steak, cubed
30–45 ml (2–3 tbsp) oil
1 large onion, diced
1 clove garlic, crushed
1 packet brown onion soup
250 ml (9 fl oz) water
seasoning to taste

Pastry
(If preferred, commercially available frozen
short pastry may be used)
500 g (1 lb 2 oz) cake flour
10 ml (2 tsp) salt
300–350 g (11–12 oz) hard margarine or butter
cold water
75 ml (5 tbsp) lemon juice
1 egg

For the filling, braise the meat in oil. Add the remaining ingredients and simmer for 30 minutes or until the meat is tender. (Add more water if it becomes too dry.) Check seasoning and adjust if necessary. Set aside to cool.

To make the pastry, sift the flour and salt into a large mixing bowl. Grate margarine or butter over the flour and work it lightly into the flour with your fingers. Using a spatula, mix in the cold water and lemon juice until the dough forms an elastic ball. Refrigerate for 30 minutes.

Grease a pie dish, approximately 24 cm (9½ in) in diameter. Divide the pastry in half and roll it out on a well-floured surface. Line the pan with one half of the pastry. Fill with meat and cover with the other half of the pastry. Press the edges down firmly with a fork and trim with a knife. Whisk the egg in a cup with 15 ml (1 tbsp) water and brush the pastry lightly with this mixture. Refrigerate the pie for about 30 minutes.

Heat the oven to 160 °C (325 °F, Gas Mark 3) and bake for 45–50 minutes. Serve with a green salad.

SOURCE UNKNOWN

Crêpes Burgundy

Serves 6

45 ml (3 tbsp) olive oil
20 pearl onions
750 g (1¾ lb) ostrich steak, cubed
45 ml (3 tbsp) flour
500 ml (18 fl oz) red wine
250 ml (9 fl oz) ostrich stock (see recipe on page 11)
45 ml (3 tbsp) tomato paste
2 ml (½ tsp) dried thyme
1 bay leaf
5 ml (1 tsp) chopped parsley
2 ml (½ tsp) coarsely ground black pepper
120 g (4 oz) button mushrooms
12 crêpes (see recipe on page 126,
or use your favourite recipe)

In a large skillet, heat the oil and sauté the onions, then remove from the pan and set aside. Add the ostrich and brown. Sprinkle flour over the meat and cook for about 2 minutes. Add the wine, stock, tomato paste, thyme, bay leaf, parsley and pepper. Reduce heat and simmer gently for 1½ hours.

Rinse the mushrooms and add them to the mixture along with the onions. Simmer for another 30 minutes.

Remove the bay leaf. Spoon the meat mixture onto the crêpes and roll them up. Serve immediately with rice pilaf.

RON HENDERSON
MAGALIES OSTRICH RANCH, KROONDAL

Stir-fried Ostrich with Litchees

Serves 4

Marinade
1 ml (¼ tsp) salt
1 ml (¼ tsp) sugar
15 ml (1 tbsp) dark soy sauce
10 ml (2 tsp) medium-dry sherry

Stir-fry
600 g (1¼ lb) ostrich steak, cut into strips
60 ml (4 tbsp) olive oil
3 large cloves garlic, cut diagonally
6 stalks celery, sliced diagonally
8 spring onions, cut diagonally
15 ml (1 tbsp) black peppercorns, coarsely crushed
15 ml (1 tbsp) brandy
1 x 765 g (1¾ lb) tin litchees, drained (and pitted)

Mix the marinade ingredients and place in a bowl with the ostrich strips. Give it a stir to coat the meat and leave to marinate for 1 hour.

Heat a wok or heavy-based pan over high heat until smoke rises. Add the oil and swirl it around to cover the surface of the wok or pan. Add the garlic and let it sizzle for a few seconds. Add the celery and spring onions and stir for a few minutes. Add the ostrich and stir-fry for about 2 minutes until just done. Add pepper and salt to taste and stir to mix.

Pour in the brandy around the edges of the wok or pan, stirring as it sizzles. Remove wok or pan from heat and spoon strips onto a serving dish. Garnish with litchees. Serve with stir-fried vegetables and steamed rice.

Source unknown

Crispy Ostrich with Stir-fried Noodles

Serves 4

1 x 85 g (3 oz) packet instant rice noodles
500 g (1 lb 2 oz) ostrich steak
10 ml (2 tsp) cornflour
10 ml (2 tsp) Five Spice
45 ml (3 tbsp) oil (peanut or sesame)
salt and freshly ground black pepper
3–4 spring onions, sliced
250 g (9 oz) bacon, diced
2 x 170 g (6 oz) tins shrimps
4 cloves garlic, chopped
small knob fresh ginger, finely chopped
2 ml (½ tsp) ground cumin
5 ml (1 tsp) curry powder
1 punnet mushrooms, sliced
15 ml (1 tbsp) soy sauce
10 ml (2 tsp) chopped fresh coriander leaves

Place the noodles in boiling water for 5 minutes. Slice the ostrich into thin, long strips and lightly dust with cornflour blended with Five Spice. In a hot pan, or preferably a wok, heat the oil. Fry 5–6 strips of steak at a time, stirring well to ensure an even, crispy texture. Place all the cooked strips onto paper towel and season with salt and pepper.

To the pan, add the spring onions, bacon, shrimps, garlic, ginger, cumin and curry powder and stir-fry for about 3 minutes. Add the well-drained and dried noodles and mushrooms and stir-fry over high heat for 3 minutes. Remove from heat and add soy sauce, crispy ostrich and the fresh coriander. Stir gently and serve immediately.

KLEIN KAROO LANDBOU CO-OPERATIVE, CHEF QUENTIN SPICKERNELL

Honeyed Ostrich Stir-fry

Serves 6

45 ml (3 tbsp) soy sauce
30 ml (2 tbsp) liquid honey
15 ml (1 tbsp) dry sherry
5 ml (1 tsp) freshly grated ginger
10 ml (2 tsp) cornflour
500 g (1 lb 2 oz) ostrich fillet, thinly sliced
30 ml (2 tbsp) sunflower oil
1 onion, sliced into rings
2 cloves garlic, crushed
4 spring onions, sliced lengthways
1 red pepper, seeded and diced
1 yellow pepper, seeded and diced
zest of 1 orange
noodles

Combine the soy sauce, honey, sherry, ginger and cornflour. Add the ostrich slices and marinate while preparing remaining ingredients.

Heat half the oil in a wok. Drain the meat, reserving the marinade. Fry the ostrich until golden brown, then remove and set aside. Sauté the onion in remaining oil and add the garlic, spring onions and peppers. Cook until the peppers are crisply tender. Add cooked ostrich and reserved marinade and heat through. Top with orange zest and serve on cooked noodles.

KLEIN KAROO LANDBOU CO-OPERATIVE

Celestial Ostrich

Serves 2

500 g (1 lb 2 oz) ostrich steak
flour
30 ml (2 tbsp) butter
2 ml (½ tsp) dried thyme
2 ml (½ tsp) dried rosemary
5 ml (1 tsp) chopped parsley
1 medium onion, finely chopped
300 g (11 oz) mushrooms
250 ml (9 fl oz) sweet white wine
5 ml (1 tsp) salt

Cut the steak in half and press flat. Roll in flour. Brown lightly in butter and sprinkle with herbs. Cover and cook slowly for 15 minutes. Add the onion, mushrooms and wine. Cover and simmer for 1 hour until tender. Season.
Serve with buttered rice.

ORIENT BUTCHERY
MAGALIESBURG

Hand-rolled Sushi

Serves 6

500 ml (2 cups) basmati or white short-grain rice
water
125 ml (4½ fl oz) rice vinegar
pinch of salt
1 sheet nori (rolled seaweed)
1 ostrich fillet
6 spring onions
6 pickled gherkins
wasabi mustard to taste
ginger to taste

Cover the rice with water and add 45 ml (3 tbsp) rice vinegar and the salt. Bring rice to a fast boil and boil for approximately 2 minutes. Cover with a tea towel and leave to steam until all the water has evaporated. Place the rice in a wooden bowl and stir in a cutting motion until it becomes glutinous. Leave to cool.

Place the sheet of nori on a damp tea towel. Cut the ostrich, spring onions and gherkins into strips.

Lay the nori on a dry cutting board and spoon the rice onto it, spreading evenly.

Make a horizontal groove where the ostrich will go. Place the fillet, onions and gherkins in the middle of the groove and season with mustard and ginger. Roll the nori Swiss roll-style and cut in the middle with a very sharp knife. Wet the knife with rice vinegar after each cut. Serve with pickled ginger, wasabi and soy sauce.

CHEF STUART FERGUSON
RUSTENBURG

Baked Ostrich with Spinach, Tomato, Brinjal and Mozzarella

Serves 6

500 g (1 lb 2 oz) ostrich fillet
3 bunches spinach
salt and freshly ground black pepper
30 ml (2 tbsp) olive oil
2 large brinjals
1 x 410 g (14 oz) tin whole peeled tomatoes
250 ml (9 fl oz) white wine
5 cloves garlic, chopped
2 ml (½ tsp) chilli sauce
10 ml (2 tsp) sweet basil
150 g (5½ oz) Mozzarella cheese, grated

Cut the fillet into 1 cm (⅜ in) thick slices and set aside. Wash and blanch the spinach, press out the water and add salt, pepper and olive oil. Cut the brinjal into 1 cm (⅜ in) thick round slices and fry lightly in a warm pan with olive oil. Set aside on some paper towel and flavour with salt and pepper. Simmer the tomatoes and white wine in the same pan until the liquid is reduced by half. Add the garlic, chilli sauce and half the herbs. Mix and remove from heat.

Make a layer of half of the brinjal, spinach, tomato and fillet slices. Arrange the rest of the vegetables in layers on top of this. Sprinkle with olive oil, Mozzarella and herbs and bake in pre-heated oven at 180 °C (350 °F, Gas Mark 4) for 20–25 minutes.

Serve with mashed potato and salad.

SOURCE UNKNOWN

Ostrich Ginger Olives

Serves 4

8 thin slices ostrich fillet or steak
vinegar
salt and freshly ground black pepper
2 ml (½ tsp) dried thyme
45 ml (3 tbsp) flour
5 ml (1 tsp) ground ginger
125 ml (½ cup) seedless raisins
1 green pepper, chopped
15–30 ml (1–2 tbsp) oil
1 packet white or brown onion soup powder,
mixed according to the packet instructions
4 cloves
1 bay leaf

Soak the meat in vinegar. Flavour with salt, pepper and thyme to taste. Tenderise. Dip the slices in flour mixed with ginger, then sprinkle raisins and green pepper over each piece. Roll the meat and pin with a toothpick. Fry in oil, then set aside and keep warm.

Pour the mixed soup into a pot with the cloves and bay leaf and bring to the boil. Discard the cloves and bay leaf and pour the gravy over the meat. Serve immediately.

SOURCE UNKNOWN

Leftover Ostrich Bake

Serves 4

500 ml (2 cups) cold, cooked, cubed ostrich meat
60 ml (4 tbsp) butter
250 ml (9 fl oz) milk
15 ml (1 tbsp) flour
15 ml (1 tbsp) Worcestershire sauce
salt to taste
1 ml (¼ tsp) cayenne pepper
grated Cheddar cheese

Braise the meat in butter, then spoon it into an ovenproof dish. Melt another spoon of butter in a pot and add milk. Bring to the boil. Add flour mixed with a dash of water and stir until smooth and boiling. Add Worcestershire sauce, salt and cayenne pepper. Pour the sauce over the meat, top with cheese and bake at 220 °C (425 °F, Gas Mark 6) for 15 minutes, then place under the grill to brown the cheese.

Serve with bean salad and sweet or mashed potatoes.

KLEIN KAROO LANDBOU CO-OPERATIVE

Red Wine, Mushroom and Ostrich Spaghetti

Serves 6

1 kg (2¼ lb) ostrich fillet, sliced into thin strips
45 ml (3 tbsp) butter
45 ml (3 tbsp) sunflower oil
1 small onion, diced
3 garlic cloves, minced
115 g (4 oz) sliced mushrooms
45 ml (3 tbsp) finely diced carrots
45 ml (3 tbsp) finely diced celery
60 ml (4 tbsp) all-purpose flour
125 ml (4½ fl oz) red wine
500 ml (18 fl oz) ostrich stock
(see recipe on page 11)
45 ml (3 tbsp) tomato paste
5 ml (1 tsp) each black pepper,
garlic powder and onion powder
450 g (1 lb) ready-made pasta
(see also recipe for pasta on page 126)
60 ml (4 tbsp) freshly grated Romano or
Parmesan cheese

In a large Dutch oven or kettle, sauté the ostrich in the butter and oil. Add the onion, garlic and vegetables and cook until tender. Sprinkle with flour, reduce heat and cook for 5 minutes.

Add the wine, stock, tomato paste and seasonings and simmer for 50 minutes, covered.

While the sauce is simmering, cook the pasta *al dente* in 2 litres (3½ pints) boiling, salted water. Drain, place on serving plates, smother with sauce and sprinkle with cheese. Serve immediately.

PAULINE HENDERSON
MAGALIES OSTRICH RANCH, KROONDAL

Ostrich Curried Biltong with Rice

Serves 30

500 g (1 lb 2 oz) pork belly fat, finely chopped
6 carrots, finely grated
3 onions, finely grated
6 kg (13 lb) ostrich biltong pieces
salt to taste
750 ml (3 cups) dried apricots, soaked overnight
and minced, or 310 ml (1¼ cups) chutney
60 ml (4 tbsp) turmeric
15 ml (1 tbsp) ginger
90 ml (6 tbsp) curry powder
2 ml (½ tsp) cayenne pepper
375 ml (13 fl oz) vinegar
90 ml (6 tbsp) sugar
60 ml (4 tbsp) cornflour
30 ml (2 tbsp) grated lemon peel
6 bay leaves
rice to serve 30 people

Combine the fat, carrots and onion and brown. Add the biltong pieces gradually, along with salt to taste. Cover and simmer for 1¼ hours, stirring every now and then.

In another pot, combine the remaining ingredients, except the rice, and cook for ten minutes. Remove bay leaves. Add the mixture to the meat and simmer for about 10 minutes. Cook the rice.

On a large platter or platters, arrange the rice in a ring and spoon the meat mixture into the centre. Garnish with parsley and serve.

Mrs A Pienaar
Hekpoort

Scrambled Ostrich Egg Omelette (page 123)

Ostrich Meat Pies (page 113)

Ostrich Meat Pies

Serves 8

1.5 kg (3¼ lb) ostrich steak, cubed
30 ml (2 tbsp) vinegar or lemon juice
2 ml (½ tsp) dried thyme, or
15 ml (1 tbsp) Tabasco sauce
7 ml (1½ tsp) nutmeg
10 ml (2 tsp) sugar
salt and freshly ground black pepper
ready-made dough
1 egg, separated

Cook the meat with vinegar and thyme for 2–3 hours. Mince all the meat and mix it with the leftover juices and the nutmeg, sugar and seasoning.

Cut circles from the dough – you will need 2 per pie. Spoon the mixture onto the bottom circle, then brush with egg white. Press down the top dough circle over the meat, brush with egg and bake at 190 °C (375 °F, Gas Mark 4) until golden brown.

SOURCE UNKNOWN

* NO SALT IS ADDED WHEN USING TABASCO SAUCE.

Ostrich Carbonara

Serves 2

120 g (4 oz) fettucine
15 g (½ oz) onions, sliced
2 cloves garlic, minced
30 g (1 oz) button mushrooms, sliced
35 g (1¼ oz) back bacon, diced
olive oil
150 ml (5¼ fl oz) fresh cream
salt and freshly ground black pepper
60 g (2 oz) ostrich fillet slices
butter
chopped chives
basil
15 g (½ oz) fresh Parmesan cheese, grated

Blanch the fettucine in boiling water, refresh under cold water and set aside. Sauté the onions, garlic, mushrooms and bacon in olive oil. Add the fettucine and cream and reduce. Season to taste.

In a separate pan, sauté the ostrich in olive oil and butter. Place the fettuccine in a bowl and stir in the sauce. Arrange the ostrich on top and sprinkle with chives. Garnish with sprig of basil and serve Parmesan cheese on the side.

CHEF CRAIG GRAVETT
SA CHEF'S ASSOCIATION

Ostrich, Bacon and Smoked Mussel Fry

Serves 4

400 g (14 oz) ostrich fillet
300 g (11 oz) bacon
¼ medium cabbage
1 plump red pepper
1 bunch spring onions
25 ml (5 tsp) sesame or peanut oil
200 g (7 oz) fresh smoked mussels
100 g (3½ oz) sprouts
25 ml (5 tsp) oyster sauce
15 ml (1 tbsp) soy sauce
10 ml (2 tsp) finely chopped ginger
5 ml (1 tsp) chilli sauce
coriander leaves to garnish

Slice the ostrich and bacon into 6 mm (¼ in) thick strips. Finely slice the cabbage, pepper and spring onions.

In a wok or large pan, heat the oil until bubbling, add the vegetables and stir vigorously for 3–4 minutes. Add the remaining ingredients and stir gently for 2 minutes. Season and serve immediately over rice or noodles and top with coriander leaves.

KLEIN KAROO LANDBOU CO-OPERATIVE, CHEF QUENTIN SPICKERNELL

Ostrich Sasheem

Serves 4

1 smoked or fresh ostrich fillet
dash of rice vinegar
15 ml (1 tbsp) soy sauce
250 ml (1 cup) fresh fruit and vegetables,
julienne style
1 clove garlic, crushed
freshly ground black pepper to taste
pickled ginger to taste
wasabi mustard to taste

Cut the fillet into paperthin slices and lay flat on a platter. Sprinkle with rice vinegar and soy sauce and decorate with fruit and vegetables.

Serve with soy sauce, garlic, black pepper, pickled ginger and wasabi mustard in separate dishes.

Use chopsticks and dip the meat into the three sauces.

CHEF STUART FERGUSON
RUSTENBURG

Offal

Ostrich Gizzard (cooked or pickled)

Serves 6

1 ostrich gizzard
6 carrots, chopped
4 onions, sliced
salt to taste

Cut the gizzard into 2 cm (¾ in) thick slices. Cook in a pressure cooker with the carrots and onions for about 30 minutes. Add salt. Reserve the meat and use the stock as a base for a soup.

Cut out the hard parts of the gizzard but don't discard. These can be minced and used as the base ingredient for a mince dish.

Serve the meat as if it were ox tongue – a light mustard sauce complements it wonderfully. Otherwise, use the meat to prepare pickled ostrich:

Pickle the slices in two parts wine vinegar to one part water, with salt and dill to taste. Leave in the refrigerator for at least 24 hours and serve as an hors d'oeuvre. It can be kept for up to 4 weeks.

DR FRITZ HUCHZERMEYER
ONDERSTEPOORT

Mock Abalone

Serves 6

1 ostrich gizzard
butter

Batter
30 ml (2 tbsp) flour
30 ml (2 tbsp) butter
250 ml (9 fl oz) milk

Remove the hard parts from the gizzard, then cut the remaining meat into thin transverse slices.

To prepare the batter, melt the butter and remove from heat. Add the flour, stirring slowly until smooth. Return to heat and cook for 2 minutes. Remove from heat. In a separate saucepan, warm the milk and slowly add this to the flour-butter mixture, stirring constantly. Return to medium heat and cook for 5 minutes.

Dip the meat slices in batter and fry in melted butter. Serve immediately.

NICK LUBBE
BEST LITTLE GUEST HOUSE, OUDTSHOORN

Ostrich Gizzard Stew

Serves 6

1 ostrich gizzard
2 onions, sliced into rings
water
salt and freshly ground black pepper to taste
5 ml (1 tsp) thyme
5 ml (1 tsp) mixed herbs
2 cloves garlic, finely chopped
125 ml (4½ fl oz) wine vinegar
30 ml (2 tbsp) chopped parsley

Prepare the gizzard by removing the membranes and hard parts. Cut it across the grain into 2 cm (¾ in) thick slices. Place a layer of meat in the bottom of a large casserole dish, cover with a thick layer of onion rings, then cover with water. Add the remaining ingredients, except the parsley.

Cover the dish and place it in a preheated oven at 150 °C (300 °F, Gas Mark 2) for 4–5 hours. Turn the meat every now and then. Add a little hot water if it shows signs of drying out.

Add the parsley just before the end of the cooking time. Taste and adjust seasoning if necessary.

Serve with rice and vegetables in a white sauce.

EUNICE UYS
BREDASDORP

Traditional Soup with Vegetables

Serves 4

¼ ostrich stomach, cut in slices
250 g (9 oz) bacon
500 ml (18 fl oz) water
250 ml (9 fl oz) white vinegar
2 carrots, sliced
1 large onion, sliced
salt and freshly ground black pepper to taste
1 ml (¼ tsp) dried thyme
1 bay leaf
3 cloves
4 peppercorns
2 tomatoes, peeled and chopped

Bring all ingredients to boil for 25 minutes in a pressure cooker, or for 3–4 hours in a normal pot. Add wine to taste and serve garnished with a sprig of parsley.

KLEIN KAROO LANDBOU CO-OPERATIVE

Cold Ostrich Stomach Salad

Serves 6

1 ostrich stomach
1.5–2 litres (2¾–3½ pints) water
5 Jamaican peppercorns
5 ml (1 tsp) dried coriander
5–10 ml (1–2 tsp) salt
freshly ground black pepper to taste
15 ml (1 tbsp) vinegar

Salad

125 ml (4½ fl oz) mayonnaise
5 ml (1 tsp) Worcestershire sauce
30 ml (2 tbsp) tomato sauce
1 small onion, grated
2 ml (½ tsp) salt
3 drops of Tabasco sauce
125 ml (½ cup) finely chopped raisins
1 green pepper, seeded and chopped
3 slices pineapple, chopped

To prepare the stomach, boil it with all the ingredients for 1–2 hours. Prick it with a skewer to ensure that it is tender. Remove the stomach from the water and set aside to cool.

To prepare the rest of the salad, cut the stomach into cubes and mix it with the salad ingredients.

Dish up on lettuce leaves and sprinkle green pepper over the top to garnish.

KLEIN KAROO LANDBOU CO-OPERATIVE

Ostrich Stomach in Curry Sauce

Serves 6

1 ostrich stomach
salt and freshly ground black pepper to taste

Sauce

3 large onions, thinly sliced
500 ml (18 fl oz) vinegar
30 ml (2 tbsp) sugar
10 ml (2 tsp) curry powder (or to taste)
5 ml (1 tsp) turmeric
½ chilli, finely chopped (optional)
6 cloves
4 peppercorns
3 lemon leaves
15 ml (1 tbsp) chutney

To prepare the sauce, fry the onions in oil until brown. Add the remaining ingredients and boil for 10 minutes.

Cook the stomach with salt and pepper until tender. Cut it into thin slices and place in the curry sauce. Cook for 4 or 5 minutes. Place in a covered dish and refrigerate for 2–3 days before use.

Can be served hot or cold.

KLEIN KAROO LANDBOU CO-OPERATIVE

Ostrich Stomach with Bacon and Ham

Serves 6

1 ostrich stomach
2 green peppers, chopped
250 g (9 oz) bacon and/or ham
15–20 ml (3–4 tsp) Tabasco sauce (no salt)
2 ml (½ tsp) freshly ground black pepper
125 ml (4½ fl oz) vinegar
15 ml (1 tbsp) sugar
5 ml (1 tsp) dried thyme

Clean the stomach with a brush and trim all the fat. Soak the stomach overnight in 30 ml (2 tbsp) lime or lemon juice mixed with 4.5 litres (8 pints) water. Rinse.

Stuff the stomach with the green peppers, bacon and ham and sew it up. Place in a pot with the remaining ingredients and cook for 3½ hours until tender. Remove from the pot and place between two plates with a weight on top. Leave overnight.

When cold, slice the stomach with a sharp knife and serve with mustard and tomatoes.

KLEIN KAROO LANDBOU CO-OPERATIVE

Italian Stomach Dish

Serves 6

1 ostrich stomach
125 ml (½ cup) minced onion
125 ml (½ cup) cooked rice
2 ml (½ tsp) dried thyme
1 ml (¼ tsp) freshly ground black pepper
30 ml (2 tbsp) sultanas
1 apple, grated
5 ml (1 tsp) lemon juice
1 egg
salt to taste
125 ml (4½ fl oz) red wine

Soak the stomach for 2 hours in 15 ml (1 tbsp) salt, 60 ml (4 tbsp) vinegar and 1 litre (1¾ pints) water. Remove and rinse with cold water.

Mix the onion, rice, thyme, pepper, sultanas, apple, lemon juice and egg and add salt. Stuff the stomach with this mixture, sew it up and cook in 500 ml (18 fl oz) water, the wine and salt and pepper to taste. Cook until tender.

Leave to cool completely, then place the stomach on a serving platter. Arrange slices of tomato and egg on the edge of the dish, top eggs with decoratively cut radishes, and garnish with green, red and yellow cocktail onions on toothpicks.

Serve with a rice salad, a mixed green salad and quince jelly.

KLEIN KAROO LANDBOU CO-OPERATIVE

Offal

Ostrich Stomach Italian Style

Serves 6

750 g (1¾ lb) ostrich stomach
275 ml (½ pint) milk mixed with 500 ml (18 fl oz) salted water
90 ml (6 tbsp) olive oil
1 large onion, sliced
100 g (3½ oz) mushrooms, chopped
1 bay leaf
30 ml (2 tbsp) tomato purée
1 clove garlic, crushed
100 ml (3½ fl oz) dry white wine or dry cider
15 ml (1 tbsp) chopped parsley
a pinch of dried rosemary or oregano
grated nutmeg
salt and freshly ground black pepper
150–300 ml (5¼–11 fl oz) ostrich stock
(see recipe on page 11), or water

Cook the stomach in milk and salted water for 1 hour, then drain and cut it into fine strips about 7.5–10 cm (3–4 in) in length.

Heat the oil in a deep pan, add the onion and, when beginning to colour, add the mushrooms. After 1 minute, add the sliced stomach.

Add the bay leaf, tomato purée, garlic and wine, herbs and spices. Season, cover pan and simmer very gently for about 1 hour until the stomach is very tender.

If the mixture shows signs of drying out, add a little stock or water from time to time. The consistency should be thick and rich.

Serve with boiled potatoes.

SOURCE UNKNOWN

Cooking with Ostrich Eggs

How much ostrich egg?

Ɐ One ostrich egg is equivalent to 22–24 hen's eggs.

Ɐ One ostrich egg, with the white and yolk beaten together, fills about 4¾ cups.

Ɐ Forty-five millilitres (3 tbsp) of ostrich egg are equal to one hen's egg.

Ɐ Ostrich egg must be beaten a good deal more than a hen's egg.

Ɐ The contents of an ostrich egg must be used within 24 hours of cracking.

Ɐ Because an ostrich egg is so much richer than a hen's egg, water or a milk/water mixture should be added.

Boiled Ostrich Egg

Serves 8

1 ostrich egg
Worcestershire sauce or tomato sauce
butter (optional)
salt and freshly ground black pepper to taste

Place a fresh ostrich egg in a saucepan filled with enough cold water to cover it completely and bring to the boil. Cook for one hour.

Serve sliced and seasoned, with slices of tomato and the sauce of your choice. Alternatively, put the white and yolk separately through a potato masher and serve on a platter, arranging the white around the yolk and adding the sauce of your choice. (When mashing the yolk, add a little butter and salt and pepper to taste.) This can be served hot or cold.

HIGHGATE OSTRICH SHOW FARM
OUDTSHOORN

Ostrich Egg Omelette

1 ostrich egg
milk, water or a milk and water mixture
salt and freshly ground pepper to taste

Beat the ostrich egg in a large bowl. Take 60 ml (4 tbsp) of the egg and place in a separate bowl. Add 15–30 ml (1–2 tbsp) milk, water or milk and water mixture. Beat again, then cook the omelette in the usual way.

This will produce an omelette for one serving. Repeat for more servings (up to 12).

SILWOOD FARM
OUDTSHOORN

Scrambled Ostrich Egg Omelette

Serves 12

120 g (4 oz) moist ostrich biltong
4 basil leaves, chopped
1 clove garlic, chopped
8 tomatoes, peeled and diced
5 ml (1 tsp) olive oil
salt and freshly ground black pepper to taste
1 ostrich egg
90 ml (6 tbsp) butter
1 onion, chopped
6 brown mushrooms
20 ml (4 tsp) white wine
75 ml (5 tbsp) milk
4 slices mosbolletjie bread (if unavailable, substitute Portuguese bread)
sprigs of basil and chopped parsley to garnish

Thinly slice the biltong and set to one side.

Combine the basil, garlic, tomatoes, oil and seasoning and place in the refrigerator to chill.

Crack the ostrich egg, whisk and strain. Heat 45 ml (3 tbsp) butter, add onion and cook. Slice and add the mushrooms, moisten with a little white wine and add seasoning. Set aside. In the same pot, add 15 ml (1 tbsp) butter and melt over low heat. Add whisked egg and milk and stir continuously over low heat until cooked.

Toast the bread, trim the crusts and serve under the scrambled egg omelette.

Arrange the tomato mixture and biltong over the eggs and garnish with basil sprigs and chopped parsley.

CHEF MARK CHARLISH
SA CHEF'S ASSOCIATION

Scrambled Ostrich Egg with Peppers

Serves 20

1 ostrich egg
oil and butter for frying
1 large onion, chopped
1 red pepper, finely chopped
1 yellow pepper, finely chopped
1 green pepper, finely chopped
Worcestershire sauce to taste
salt and freshly ground black pepper to taste

Beat the egg well for at least 10 minutes.

Heat the oil and butter in a large, heavy skillet and sauté the onion until translucent. Add the peppers and cook over medium heat for 5 minutes. Add Worcestershire sauce, seasoning and egg. Scramble and serve immediately.

DANELLE COULSON
HEKPOORT

Ostrich Egg Fruitcake

1 kg (2¼ lb) butter or margarine
1.2 kg (2¾ lb) sugar
1 ostrich egg, separated
250 ml (9 fl oz) milk
1.2 kg (2¾ lb) cake flour
15 ml (1 tbsp) salt
10 ml (2 tsp) cream of Tartar
500 g (1 lb 2 oz) dates
250 g (9 oz) cherries
250 g (9 oz) mixed peel
375 g (13 oz) sultanas
375 g (13 oz) currants
5 ml (1 tsp) bicarbonate of soda
250 ml (9 fl oz) brandy

Cream the butter, sugar, egg yolk and milk. Sift the flour, salt and cream of Tartar. Mix all the fruit with the bicarbonate of soda. Add the fruit to the flour and egg mixture. Mix thoroughly. Add the well-beaten egg white and brandy.

Use a box about 40 x 25 cm (16 x 9¾ in) in size, reinforced with four rows of strong string. Line the box with foil and three layers of brown paper. Butter the last layer of paper and pour the cake mixture into the box.

Bake at 180 °C (350 °F, Gas Mark 4) for 45 minutes, then at 160 °C (325 °F, Gas Mark 3) for 1 hour. To prevent the top of the fruitcake becoming too crusty, place another layer of brown paper on top.

Leave in the box for 10 minutes and let it cool on a wire rack. When cool, cut the fruitcake into four blocks and store until ready to be served.

MRS C M NORTIER
OUDTSHOORN

Sponge Cake

200 ml (7 fl oz) well-beaten ostrich egg
500 ml (2 cups) sugar
500 ml (2 cups) flour
25 ml (5 tsp) baking powder
a pinch of salt

Beat the egg and sugar briskly for 15 minutes. Combine the flour, baking powder and salt and add it to the egg mixture. Mix thoroughly. Pour into a greased baking tin (about a 22 cm/8¾ in diameter) and bake at 200 °C (400 °F, Gas Mark 6) for about 1 hour or until a wooden skewer comes out clean.

Turn out onto a cooling rack. Serve with apricot jam.
This recipe can also be used to make trifle or rusks.

Mrs C M Nortier
Oudtshoorn

Ostrich Egg Mousse

Serves 15–20

25 ml (5 tsp) gelatine, sprinkled over
150 ml (5¼ fl oz) water and 60 ml (4 tbsp) lemon juice
2 large English cucumbers, thinly sliced
75 ml (5 tbsp) gelatine
250 ml (9 fl oz) dry white wine
500 ml (18 fl oz) Béchamel sauce
375 ml (13 fl oz) cream, whipped
25 ml (5 tsp) Worcestershire sauce
salt and freshly ground black pepper to taste
1 hard-boiled ostrich egg, grated
60 ml (4 tbsp) lemon juice
edible flowers and salad leaves to decorate

Heat the gelatine, water and lemon juice mixture to dissolve the gelatine. Pour into the base of one very large tin measuring about 35 cm (14 in) in diameter or use two smaller ones. Garnish with cucumber slices.

Sprinkle the 75 ml (5 tbsp) gelatine over the wine and heat to dissolve the gelatine.

Combine the cold Béchamel sauce with the cream, Worcestershire sauce and seasonings. Add the egg and lemon juice, then add the gelatine mixture and allow to cool slightly. Pour the mixture into the tins and place in the refrigerator to set.

To unmould, dip the tins in boiling water for a few seconds, then gently shake the tin to loosen the mousse. Turn out onto a serving platter and garnish with flowers and salad leaves.

Source unknown

Basic Pasta

Serves 40

6 kg (13½ lb) semolina flour
15 ml (1 tbsp) salt
1 ostrich egg
90 ml (6 tbsp) oil
500 ml (18 fl oz) ice-cold water

Sift the flour and salt together and place in a very large mixing bowl. Beat the egg and slowly blend it into the flour mixture. Slowly add the oil and water until a smooth, soft dough has formed.

Knead the dough for 15 minutes, then leave to rest for an additional 15 minutes. Roll out the dough – it is best to do this a quarter at a time. Lightly dust with flour, fold in three and roll out again. Repeat this about six to eight times, using just enough flour to prevent the dough from sticking to the roller.

Pass the dough through a pasta machine, gradually setting the rollers down until you have reached the desired thickness. The result should be a smooth sheet of dough that is ready to process as you require.

Pass the dough through a pasta machine or cut by hand to the desired size. If processed by hand, simply roll the dough and cut into thin strips for noodles (fettucine) or into wider strips for lasagne, cannelloni, ravioli, etc.

If not using the pasta immediately, store it in an airtight container in the refrigerator and use within 2 weeks.

PAULINE HENDERSON
MAGALIES OSTRICH RANCH, KROONDAL

Ostrich Egg Crêpes

Serves 6

250 ml (1 cup) all-purpose flour
1 ml (¼ tsp) salt
30 ml (2 tbsp) oil
250 ml (9 fl oz) milk
60 ml (4 tbsp) soda water
45 ml (3 tbsp) whisked ostrich egg
2 ml (½ tsp) vanilla essence

Sift the flour and salt together. Blend in the oil, milk and water and add the whisked egg to the mixture. Stir in the vanilla. Beat until a smooth, thin batter has formed.

To cook the crêpes, spread about 45 ml (3 tbsp) batter in a lightly buttered hot skillet. Cook for about 1½ minutes, turn the crêpe and cook for 1 minute over medium heat. Turn out and use as required.

DANELLE COULSON
HEKPOORT

VARIATION: Instead of plain soda water, use blackcurrant (or any other flavour) sparkling water.

Index

Entries followed by an asterisk (*) indicate those that have been photographed.